# CROWN & SWORD

SPIRITUAL TRAINING FOR BECOMING
A ROYAL WARRIOR

CHRISTINE JAYNES

All Bible verses were taken from NIV unless otherwise noted.

The Holy Bible, New International Version, NIV

Copyright© 1973,1978,1984, 2011 by Biblica, Inc. Published by Zondervan, Grand Rapids, Michigan 49530 USA

Scripture quotations marked (NLT) are taken from the *Holy Bible*, New Living Translation, copyright ©1996. Used by permission of Tyndale House Publishers, Inc, Wheaton Illinois 60189 All rights reserved.

Scripture taken from THE MESSAGE. Copyright © 1993, 1994, 1995, 1996, 2000, 2001, 2002. Used by permission of NavPress Publishing Group.

All Greek and Hebrew words - definitions and translations from BlueLetterBible.org. Strong's Greek Lexicon or Vine's Expository Dictionary. *Blue Letter Bible is a 501(c)(3) nonprofit organization* https://www.blueletterbible.org/

More references located at the end of Book

This book was improved & edited by Jenna Hermle

The Royal Warrior gracing the cover was painted by the talented artist Rebekah Hamilton.

# ENDORSEMENTS

·  ·  ·  ·  ·  ·  ·  ·  ·  ·

**What Leaders say about Crown & Sword:**

"Because I am a real advocate of mentoring women, I see this study as a great tool. If one were to answer the questions and openly share them with a mentor; I think positive change could happen.

Christine is a committed learner of the Word. She exhibits a healthy balance of personal investment and family investment which has enabled this study to come to fruition."

*~Sherri Holdridge (Pastor's wife, mentor and writer)*

In *Crown & Sword*, Christine Jaynes has formed a study that is both timely and timeless, with the ability to impact and nudge the heart of the reader towards God's heart and vision for them. The combination of her unique voice and perspective, her vulnerability in sharing her own experience and insights, and the scriptural foundation that is clear at every corner, she will help to guide the reader towards the empowerment that comes with realizing the true identity that God has placed inside us. Not one of fear, but one of power, love, and a sound mind.

*~Marty Wheeler (Youth and Worship Pastor)*

"My opinion is that younger women will benefit from *Crown & Sword*, and with the help of the Holy Spirit, will experience the author's love for the Lord. I also believe that older women will find themselves opened up to new possibilities as they look back on their years of experience and combine what they've learned with a new zeal to live it and pass it on to others. Doing the workbook assignments won't be easy—especially if done by the Spirit—but it will be profitable for spiritual maturity and fruitfulness. And that's how our Father in heaven is glorified, as Jesus stated it in John 15:8.

Many blessings to those who decide to go through this training…"

*~Bill Holdridge (Calvary Chapel Pastor, Poimen Ministries)*

For more information about Christine's ministry visit Christinejaynes.com

# THE "THANK YOU" PAGE

• • • • • • • • • •

Thank you.

Thank you to the man in my world who has walked through the last 13 years with me faithfully.

Who has seen me fail and break. Who has endured my excentricities, both good and bad.

I'm deeply grateful for all the support and affection you give as I pursue the call on my life.

David Jaynes, you are a very good man.

Thank you Cooper, Tyler, Sam & Joe

for making this journey with me and investing into the kingdom by supporting your momma.

Daddy, thank you for your tireless support and your unending affirmations.

Thank you Red Tent Originals & Titus Project. You ladies know how it's meant to be.

Discipleship in it's true authentic form. Thank you for showing me how it's done!

Thank you Jenna Hermle. Your gracious dedication to this project was astounding.

Thank you for sharing your gifts so generously. I can't wait to see how God rewards you…

Rebekah Hamilton!

The painting God graced Crown & Sword with through you're phenomenal talent is breathtaking.

So excited to see God grant you all the desires of your heart!

(find Rebekah at rreneeimperfections.com)

Thank you Jon Trujillo for blessing me/us with your Tech talents!

# ABOUT THE AUTHOR

**CHRISTINE JAYNES IS PASSIONATE ABOUT RELATIONSHIPS -** the one thing we take into eternity.

Those relationships most important to her are with her husband, David, and her four growing boys. The Jaynes family lives in the Yuba-Sutter area of Northern California. Christine spent her childhood in several different Northern California locations. Her high school and young adult stomping grounds were in the Boulder, Colorado area.

Christine started doing ministry at the age of 18 at Flatirons Church in Lafayette, Colorado when it was just beginning. This is where she started developing her passion for discipleship!

She also enjoys being outside, spoken word, acting, and witnessing the beauty of women doing life together.

"Seasons of life can often leave women feeling defeated. I believe in empowering women to live victoriously through God's Word. Discipleship makes Scripture practical and therefore applicable."

# THE VISION

• • • • • • • • • •

A dreary gray paints the sky and the smell of rain refusing to fall fills the air.

The battle is raging in a large valley spread out before you.

Ringing across the field are sounds of clashing swords and cries.

Cries of pain. Cries of defeat. Cries of effort. Cries of victory.

Standing out in the chaos is a strong and elegant woman with

beautiful hair flowing from under her helmet.

Loosening her sword from something bloody she looks up so that her features become clear.

Her face is beauty defined-

holding eyes that are both hard and soft at the same time,

blushed with both dirt and blood somehow radiating pure cleanliness.

Full lips rest together gently, yet in their silence you sense the power they hold.

Applying herself to the task at hand, her sweat smells strangely sweet.

Focusing only on what's going on right around her,

She fights her own battles,

Yet occasionally lashing out she dismembers something

about to hurt someone beside her.

"Who is she?" you ask? She's You.

This powerful, strong, disciplined, and beautiful woman--

She's *YOUR* personality, heart, and mind, made by the great God.

She's equipped with a power that comes from the mighty Holy Spirit,

a power accessed through the blood of Christ.

All of her is intimately entwined with the Trinity and

this makes her fierce and breathtaking.

Regal and agile, this woman is both royalty and athlete.

Both a Queen and a Warrior. She is you.

If you are a woman, if the great God is Lord of your life

and Jesus Christ is your Savior, then you are a Royal Warrior.

What kind of Royalty are you? What kind of a Warrior are you?

Let us eagerly respond to the title God has given us and be all that He made us to be.

Let's join ranks to impact God's kingdom in a mighty way.

# TABLE OF CONTENTS

• • • • • • • •

In this curriculum, you will break open God's Word, and break through any misconceptions about the royal title given to Believers and what we, as Warriors, are called to do.

> *There is no fear in the Spirit that God has given us. In part one, we will identify some of the things that trigger fear. We will also establish the truth of who God has made us to be as the truth that reigns in us, thus dethroning and renouncing fear in our lives.*

**PART II: BE POWERFUL** ......................................................................... 23
**Participate in the spirit of power:**

*God has given us power and authority in Christ. Here we will learn how to participate, practically and actively, by exercising that power in our lives.*

**PART IV: THE DISCIPLINED WARRIOR** ..................................89
**Engage in the battle:**

*We must respond to the call God has put on our lives with the authority and power with which He has graced us. Let's put our hands to the work. May God's purpose for us be lived out to the fullest!*

> "God did not give us
> a spirit of timidity,
> but a spirit of power and of
> love and of a sound mind."
>
> ~2 Timothy 1:7~

· · · · · · · · ·

## MISSION:

Part I: Renounce the spirit of fear

Part II: Participate in the spirit of power

Part III: Embrace the royal title

Part IV: Engage in the battle

# Your Mission, Should you Choose to Accept

· · · · · · · · ·

" Thinking will not overcome fear, but action will."
W. Clement Stone

I'M SO HONORED THAT YOU'VE CHOSEN TO PICK UP *CROWN & Sword*. Thank you for investing in it! I pray that God will use this material to draw you closer to Himself, and that the investment of your time, energy, and finances will bring an abundant return!

My hope is that you will respond to the challenge this curriculum presents with a growing passion for God's kingdom. I pray that you will meet each assignment with anticipation for God's Spirit to move in you, as you persevere and follow through with each section.

If you are ready to renounce fear and press onto successful spiritual life, it will be hard. Overcoming fear is not easy, and neither is walking in love, power, and discipline.

But it does feel miraculous to stand triumphant in your kingdom. To know you've accomplished a hard thing and to have experienced God in new, intimate ways.

Every action you take toward overcoming fear and becoming the Royal Warrior you were made to be is worth it. We don't take much into eternity. Most of what we do with our lives here on earth is temporal. Yet relationships last forever. The time and energy you put into your relationship with God has an eternal return. This return is not limited to a solid and eternal foundation with the Trinity; by becoming someone who walks intimately with God, every other earthly relationship improves as well. *Eternity* will be better because of the time and energy you invest into knowing God now.

· · · · · · ·

This curriculum is broken into four parts. It is structured around 2 Timothy 1:7, which states, *"For God has not given us a spirit of fear and timidity, but of power, love and self-discipline." (NLT)*

In part 1, we will examine and renounce fear by pursuing a balanced perspective.

In part 2, we will examine the power that God has given us and discover how to participate in it, practically applying it to our daily lives.

In part 3, we will examine love by studying the relationships God has given us in His trinity and by exploring the types of love that are mentioned in Scripture.

And in part 4, we will discuss discipline and how to live out our victory in the day to day of our lives.

As you proceed with this material, decide what you can commit to and follow through. The curriculum is set up so that it can be flexible to fit whatever schedule your season requires.

The material is very versatile and can be used in endless ways.

Leaders, teachers or small group facilitators can use this curriculum as lesson plans, mentors can use this material to provoke intentional and productive conversations, and an individual can use the material to further their understanding of both God and themselves.

There are several "Digging Deeper" sections under each lesson, which are meant to help deepen understanding and application of the concept being taught. Any Digging Deeper could also turn into its own lesson, just by investigating further into the context of the Scripture and breaking it down.

This curriculum can be done individually, but I highly recommend gathering a community of women with whom you can process the material and encourage one another, while applying yourself to the work. This community approach would also provide some accountability.

Here are some options on how the material can be used:

**As an individual:**

**Option 1:** Use each chapter as a weekly study. The teaching can be used as a weekly introduction, and the Digging Deeper prompts as daily exercises through the week.

**Option 2:** Commit to spend a specific amount of time in the material daily, without putting a deadline on when the questions need to be answered. (These questions are not meant to be rushed.)

**Option 3:** Plan to do one chapter per month. Part 1 alone would then provide 6 months worth of study. This would allow you to spend a week or so on each Digging Deeper, giving you time to research context and the original Greek. This option might also provide material for someone teaching a weekly study.

**As a Leader/Teacher:**

**Option 1:** Use each chapter as a weekly study. The chapters content can be used as a conversation starter, a devotional offering, or a lesson and the Digging Deeper prompts can be handed out as "homework".

**Option 2:** Use each "Digging Deeper" as a lesson. Research the content of the scripture, dig into the Greek and expand on the prompts to create a lesson with your own epiphanies and experiences to expanding on the concepts and verses.

Of course, there are more options. You, your group, or your class have the freedom to decide how to apply this curriculum to your lives.

Use the "Mission Accepted" page to write out your commitment and then prayerfully sign it, making a promise to yourself and your God to follow through.

I pray that you allow the Spirit to teach, grow, strengthen, and sustain you through your work.

Fear, love, discipline, and power are hard things to tackle. Let's do this well and do it right. Be diligent in your journaling: write out your work and your prayers. Renewing the mind and setting it on truth takes effort. Studies show that when you write things down, you are much more likely to remember them.

*The Message* paraphrases James 1:22-25 saying:

> "Don't fool yourself into thinking you are a listener when you are anything but, letting the Word go in one ear and out the other. Act on what you hear! Those who hear and don't act are like those who glance in the mirror, walk away, and two minutes later have no idea who they are, what they look like.
>
> But whoever catches a glimpse of the revealed counsel of God - the free life! - even out of the corner of his eye, and sticks with it, is no distracted scatterbrain but a man or woman of action. That person will find delight and affirmation in the action."

## DIGGING DEEPER 1

........................................................

### James 1:22-25

1. Prayerfully write out a commitment to yourself and God about completing this study. (Page 14 provides an optional worksheet to do this!)

2. Create a plan for follow-through. Write it out in order to be sure that you are not just looking at this curriculum that points you toward the Word, and then the next moment forgetting the truth you just received.

## DIGGING DEEPER 2

........................................................

### Hebrews 12:1-3

1. What are some sins that you need to throw off in order to not be entangled on this leg of your race?

2. In what ways can you fix your eyes on Jesus, the pioneer and **_perfecter_** of our faith today?

3. Consider the joyous reward Jesus had set before Him, motivating Him to suffer the way He did. Record your thoughts.

4. What are things that you can think about that would give you joy and hope in persevering in whatever season you're in right now?

5. How have you grown to be better through previous seasons of persevering?

## DIGGING DEEPER 3

........................................................

### Hebrews 10:36-39

1. How is it evident in your life that you need to persevere to do the will of God?

2. Why is it worth it to you to persevere in the will of God to receive what He has promised? Explain your answer.

3. List some of God's promises to you.

4. Describe what a righteous person living by faith looks like.

5. Record some thoughts you have about being a person in whom God takes pleasure.

........

## DIGGING DEEPER 4

........................................................

**Hebrews 11:6**

1. The fact that you are working through this curriculum is evidence that you are earnestly seeking God. What are the expectations you have for yourself and for God at the time of completing the work of *Crown & Sword*?

2. Before proceeding, examine the practicality of your expectations regarding your time commitment and make any necessary adjustments.

3. How are you expressing your faith today? Rest assured that your God is pleased.

4. Identify a time when you didn't follow through with a commitment that you should have, and compare it to a time that you did complete a commitment and felt victorious.

# MISSION ACCEPTED

*I commit to:*

_____

Signature Required

# PART I

# BALANCING CLAY

. . . . . . . . . .

God did not give us a spirit of fear.

## THE MISSION:

*Renounce Fear By Embracing Truth*

. . . . . . . . .

# CHAPTER 1:

# EQUILIBRIUM

• • • • • • • • • •

"Be stubborn about your goals, and flexible about your
methods."
Unknown

"ROYAL WARRIOR." SEEMS LIKE A CONTRADICTION, DOESN'T
it?

Honestly, as I've studied the Scriptures and wrestled with living according to them, I've found myself asking, "Am I to run the race, or be still? Embrace discipline or walk in freedom? Be obedient or cling to grace?"

How does one do both? Is it possible to run and be still at the same time? To be disciplined in freedom and obedient in grace?

It has been said that "Mankind will never cease striving to find balance."

God says all things are possible through Him, and He has instructed us to balance racing and stillness, discipline and freedom, obedience and grace. The temptation, though, is to try to make it an exact science, to discover the precise equilibrium between it all.

For years I'd pray, "Lord, how do I embody graceful royalty, possessing peaceful authority and also live as an active warrior fervently fighting for your glory?"

In His response to me, He revealed that I need to first BE and then DO. First, BE HIS. Then DO everything He has set before me, as the unique creation He made me to be.

• • • • • • • •

3

The spirit of fear, in contrast, would state, "You must *do* everything well in order to *be* who God made you to be."

In the midst of wrestling through the *doing* and *being* in my life, there was a day when God stated: "Christine, you are still the same lump of clay I started out with."

The truth is, I'm not the exact same female I was when I was 5, 16, or 25-- I've grown and been re-formed. The Potter's hands were shaping that five-year-old girl, rounding out that 16-year-old, and softening that 25-year-old. I'm a whole different form than I was when God first put His Spirit into me at age 11 - BUT I'm still the same clay. I'm still made up of the same material He started with; I am *not* the jobs and different callings on my life. Instead, those jobs and callings are paths that change throughout the seasons of my life as I walk out my unique contribution to the eternal story.

A lump of clay isn't anything special until it is formed into something. In order to create equilibrium in ourselves, we work with our Lord, allowing Him to mold the clay from which we were created, and then apply ourselves to what we are made for.

## DIGGING DEEPER 5

### 1 Corinthians 9:24-27 & Psalm 37:7

1. When do you find yourself "running aimlessly", without purpose?

2. Define "the prize" and why it's worth beating your body to attain it.

3. Do you ever "strike a blow" to your body making it your "slave"? If you do, define your reason for doing so. What prize are you looking for when you take this action?

4. Identify a difference between someone "being still before the Lord, waiting patiently for Him" (Psalm 37:7) and someone "running aimlessly" or a "boxer beating the air."

5. I have heard that waiting is an action word. Do you agree? Do you think it possible to "be still before the Lord" while "running in a way to get the prize"? How does one do such a thing?

## DIGGING DEEPER 6

### Numbers 32:27 & Psalm 46:9-10

1. Is there a place in your life where you have been given instruction and you need to follow through to "fight before the Lord"?

2. While Psalm 46 is likely referencing how God will make wars cease at the end of time, think about how He has already won the victory and that victorious peace can actually dwell in you **now**, because of Christ. Where in your world do you hear God speaking the words, "Be still, and know that I am God"?

## DIGGING DEEPER 7

### 1 Timothy 6:12 & Exodus 14:14

1. How can you "fight the good fight of faith" today?

2. What does it look like to "take hold" of the eternal life while living and functioning in this non-eternal body?

3. Where in the past have you seen the Lord fight for you?

4. Do you have a tendency to fight things in your flesh while forgetting to be still and allow the Lord to fight? Identify any habits that distract you from allowing the Lord to work out His deliverance, in His way.

# CHAPTER 2

# BE THE CLAY

• • • • • • • • • •

"Have no fear of perfection- you'll never reach it."
Unknown

AS I PRESSED INTO GOD'S WORDS ABOUT BEING THE CLAY, I learned that this thought takes us back to the very beginning of creation.

In the beginning when God made the heavens and the earth, when He scooped up dirt to make the first human - He had you and me in mind. He gave us unique personalities. He gave us passions, with certain likes and dislikes. And then He placed us at a certain point in history as part of the eternal story.

Genesis 2:7 says, "The Lord God formed the man from the dust of the ground and breathed into his nostrils the breath of life." And Isaiah 64:8 says, "We are the clay, you are the Potter, we are all the work of your hands."

The very definition of clay states that it comes from the ground! "Clay comes from the ground… it is made from minerals, plant life and animals, all the ingredients of soil." ("Clay and Pottery" by Phylilis McKnee)

Our balancing comes down simply to this: being the clay we were created to be.

How many times do we look at those around us and try to be like them? We admire something about another person and try to make their passion our own because of how lovely it looks on

• • • • • • •

them. We think "surely it will look that good on us." The spirit of fear says we aren't as good as they are and that our value is therefore less.

The reality is, God doesn't need you to fill that role. That other person you admire is already filling it. You were made to fill a certain place in history that nobody else can. He made you the way He did - with all your likes, dislikes, desires, and passions - because <u>He wants you to function in them</u>! There is so much freedom in this truth!

Let's take David's cue and delight in the way God designed us: "I praise you because I am fearfully and wonderfully made!" (Ps 139:14) God did not fail in any way when He formed you. He did a marvelous job. Don't fear that God somehow "messed up" when He made you. It is impossible for God to fail.

In Ephesians 2, God says we are His masterpiece. In her book *A Million Little Ways,* Emily Freeman breaks down this word "poiema", the Greek word for "poem":

"God calls you his workmanship, his poiema. What happens when God writes poetry?

We do. We happen. We are walking poetry, the kind that moves, the kind who has hands and feet, the kind with mind, will and emotion. We are what happens when God expresses himself."

## DIGGING DEEPER 8

**2 Corinthians 3:17**

1. Do you know your personality type? If you do, do a refresher and read up on your personality again; if you don't, take a test and learn about it. (Truity.com or 16 personalities.com have free tests!) This is important to help identify the unique ways in which you were made.

2. Do you ever finding yourself trying to be something you're not? Write out and explain your answer. Is there any sense of freedom when you think of how God made you and that He had a purpose for making you that way?

## DIGGING DEEPER 9

**Galatians 5:1**

1. Where in your life do you feel like the yoke of slavery may be threatening you?

2. How can you "stand firm" and avoid this burden of slavery?

3. Write a list of your strengths and weaknesses.

4. What weaknesses can you celebrate where the Lord is working and making you stronger?

5. How would you define "freedom" in your life?

## DIGGING DEEPER 10

### James 2:12-13

1. In your own words, define "the law that brings freedom."

2. How does one act and speak in a way that recognizes that law?

3. Make a list of your likes and dislikes. (Reading, cooking, hiking, playing with kids, etc.) Recognize that these things are part of how God specifically made you.

4. At what times do you find that you don't have mercy on yourself? Howcanmercy triumph judgment in your life?

5. How does giving yourself mercy while recognizing your personality, likes/dislikes, and strengths and weaknesses allow you to extend mercy to others?

# CHAPTER 3:

# POUNDING CLAY

. . . . . . . . . .

"The greatest fear that people live in is the fear of what other people think."
David Icke

NOW THAT WE'VE GOT A GOOD GRASP ON THE WAY GOD HAS made us, let's make a distinction between our fleshly desires and our God-given desires. I've struggled in the past, denying myself what I desired because I believed the lie that **all** my desires are fleshly and selfish. The spirit of fear told me I needed to work off a checklist to be who I was called to be - and I was selfish if I ever desired anything different.

The truth, however, is that many of our desires are actually God-given. And He wants us to function *in* them.

Perhaps like me, you have found that you've allowed others to convince you that you're not as you should be, both when they intended to do so and even when they had no such inclination.

The spirit of fear can make a human interpretation of Scripture seem more important than the Spirit's prompting, more important than actually stepping forth and being like Jesus. Fear might bind us with law.

2 Corinthians 3:6 says "the letter kills but the spirit gives life." This might explain why we try to use the letter (Scripture) to pound our clay (or someone else's) into something that we think looks better. "And woe to you experts in the law, woe to you, because you load people down with burdens

. . . . . . . . .

9

they can hardly carry, and you yourselves will not lift one finger to help them." Luke 11:46 (NIV) There are times when we will be a victim of this tendency, while at other times we will be guilty of it.

Luke 11:43 says "Woe to you Pharisees, because you give God a tenth of your mint, rue and all other kinds of garden herbs, but you neglect justice and the love of God. **You should have practiced the latter without leaving the former undone**."

The Scriptures lay out many guidelines for how we are to live in accordance with God's will. But we know that God cannot be contained in a book. He is more than the Bible.

I believed for years that the Bible was black and white, with maybe some gray areas that gave us a bit of freedom. I've come to discover, however, how very colorful the Word of God is. How it moves and breathes and meets us in the very depths of our unique core.

I love the imagery of our clay being molded by the Potter, allowing the Spirit who brings life to gently work the Word into us. In contrast, when we take the Word in our own hands and pound it into our being, trying to make ourselves different, we are actually choosing legalism. We make our lists of what we need to do, like the Pharisees, and then we do them, checking things off along the way. We humbly think how "helpful" we are to God, and how we are earning a place that is closer to His heart. When we try to pound ourselves into being a certain way, though, we forget that God is a God of love and justice, that He's not looking for the sacrifices of worship. He wants the **worshiper**. He wants to mold our clay a certain way so that HE can fill it.

When God is molding us, it might hurt, like discipline or pruning, but His gentle hand is the one doing it, and He comforts us along the way.

Satan knows the Scripture and can twist it ever so slightly into a lie. Once this deception is made, we can go around for years denying chunks of our God-given identity while believing, "I'm standing in truth - because it's what the Bible says." Actually, though, we are standing on an interpretation of "the letter that kills."

Sisters, this is one big reason why we must never lean too heavily on one teacher. We need to make sure we are drawing from God's Word and learning new things from a number of different sources. We, the church, were made to work together and balance each other out. One teacher we love might have a great emphasis on grace. Praise Jesus! We desperately need to know grace well! However, we must also have a teacher (or other source) that is constantly challenging us to behave in greater obedience and strive to give our absolute utmost for our great God.

It has been a process for me to embrace the great freedom of how our likes and dislikes are part of who God made us to be. Not only do my personality and my upbringing bias me toward legalistic discipline, for example, but I also drew from many sources that were bent that way. It was important for me to dig into some teaching that helped balance this bias.

Of course, as we gain knowledge of this freedom, we mustn't forget that there is such thing as fleshly desire, and we can even misuse Scripture to support such indulgences. This is something to keep in mind as we celebrate how God made us.

We'll discuss discipline in greater detail later--because even though our personality might not like to do dishes, it doesn't mean we're off the hook for doing them.

The kind of woman we are, and the way we creatively apply ourselves to the tasks at hand in order to bring God glory, **this** is our purpose and the whole reason we were created.

## DIGGING DEEPER 11

### Ephesians 2:8-10

1. How can this verse be translated to "you're off the hook"?

2. How do other people's expectations of you, both explicitly communicated or implied, create insecurities and doubts?

3. How do your own expectations impact those doubts and insecurities?

## DIGGING DEEPER 12

### Isaiah 45:9-12

1. What are some quarrels you may have picked with your Maker regarding His design of you?

2. Have you ever felt the need to quench a desire in your heart because you thought it was fleshly, when really it was a desire that God had intentionally put there? Is there any place in your heart that might need to experience the law of freedom now?

3. Do you ever find yourself thinking or saying things about others that may insult the One who made them? Define those times and repent of the moments when this has happened in the past, and be ready to repent of any other instances that might happen in the future.

## DIGGING DEEPER 13

### 1 Corinthians 12:4-31

1. How does this passage inspire you to celebrate yourself?

2. When are there times that you are tempted to think that because you are weak in one area, that you don't belong in the body of Christ at all?

3. Anybody can relate to this, because everyone has a body and experiences the necessity of it working together. Everyone has also experienced discomfort when the body doesn't all work together. Describe a time when part of your body wasn't working right and how it affected the rest of your body.

4. Describe a time when someone in your life was hurting and how that affected you.

5. Describe the different ways that you've witnessed others gather around someone who was hurting, each person offering a different set of giftings.

## DIGGING DEEPER 14

### Galatians 5:13-18

1. Compare verses 13 & 18. "You were called to be free… but do not indulge" versus "but if you are led by the Spirit you are not under law." We are not under law, yet we mustn't indulge in laziness, gossip, crudeness, cruelty, lust, gluttony… the list is more extensive in verses 19-20. Are you using your freedom responsibly?

2. How can we *not* gratify the desires of the flesh?

# CHAPTER 4:

# IN WALKS INIQUITY

· · · · · · · · ·

"You were perfect in your ways from
the day you were created,
till iniquity was found in you."
Ezekiel 28:15

THE ROOT OF FEAR IS LIES, AND LIES ARE BIRTHED FROM Satan. In order to live in truth, free from fear, we must first acknowledge fear's source.

Once there was a magnificent angel named Lucifer who was "perfect in his ways" until iniquity was found in him.

```
Iniquity (noun) - vice, evil, sin, villainy, criminality; odiousness,
atrocity, egregiousness; outrage, monstrosity, obscenity, reprehensi-
bility. (Oxforddictionary.com)
```

Iniquity sounds like the right word. Ever since Lucifer was cast to earth and renamed Satan, iniquity has run rampant in our world.

Satan is here to steal, kill, and destroy and he wants to reap as much destruction as possible. He is the father of lies, and his desire is to destroy whatever work the Lord, the Father of all truth, is doing. This liar wants to cause as much damage as he can before he is brought down by our great God, and since we are God's valuable possession, he aims at us.

The above definition of iniquity included this quote: "Many runaways become the pawns of iniquity."

· · · · · · · ·

You might have experienced this reality: when we are being deceived, we don't know it. And it doesn't help that Satan disguises himself to still be an angel of light. We become a pawn of what (or who) is deceiving us. Sound abusive? It is. Let's fight back by working on this renouncing of fear and dismissing lies.

So how do you even know that you are being deceived?

For a start, fear can be a sign that deception is at work in your world.

Satan wants us to think he's more powerful than we are--and he actually accomplishes that a lot of the time. God's truth, however, tells us that we possess the power that raised Christ from the grave, and that we have absolute power over the devil. But Satan wants to make us afraid. He wants us to fear circumstances, to fear inadequacy, to fear people and institutions. He will do whatever he can to make us fear anything with a "delia" fear. "Delia" is the Greek word used for "fear" in 2 Timothy 1:7, and it refers to a curse of the flesh filled with torment (blueletterbible.com). That is certainly not what God gave us.

So whenever you start to feel a "deliah" fear, the first step is to examine what you are believing and which one of your beliefs might be stemming from a lie.

You can prevent deception and fear by praying against deceit, pray that God would bring any lies in your life into the light.

We must also learn to distinguish between facts and truth. They are not the same. Facts deal with circumstances, while truth deals with the Word of God. Facts are only a small factor when it comes to God's power and plan.

Fear magnifies facts into mountains that can't be moved or climbed. As a royal member of God's family, we know better. But sometimes we forget; we buy into the lie, we settle in with the fear, and we find ourselves overcome by the mountains that are just facts.

Fear can also drive us to complacency, or it might drive us to coping by using unhealthy outlets that seem harmless. Harmless actions driven by fear can destroy us.

Yet the power of God brings beauty from ashes. No matter what we've done or how destructive our actions have been, our God can take the ugliest thing and cover it with His mercy, grace, power, and glory until it becomes breathtakingly gorgeous.

Sisters, we have an enemy. He is by no means as powerful as God and even we are more powerful than he is once we are equipped with the Holy Spirit, but he is still a very real and dangerous force. God has told us to be on our guard against him.

He was cast down from Heaven because he believed he was greater than God. He convinced one third of the angels to join him in trying to usurp our Lord. Because of this sin, both he and his followers were cast down. He is the bully in this world and the true enemy who uses people as his pawns. Although he can't read your mind, he knows your patterns and what you're drawn to. He knows what distracts you, he knows how to make evil look appealing to you, and he knows how to accuse you, make you feel inferior, and intimidate you. "Delia" is a weapon of the enemy, but the glory be to God, it is a weapon we are fully able to defeat!

## DIGGING DEEPER 15

**Luke 10:18-20**

1. Imagine the scene of Jesus with his Father, witnessing Satan falling from heaven. Record any thoughts you have regarding verse 18.

2. Have you ever encountered satanic power? Have you ever caught a glimpse into the unseen spiritual realm and witnessed any of Satan's havoc?

3. Prayerfully record your thoughts about having authority to overcome all the power of the enemy.

## DIGGING DEEPER 16

**Matthew 8:23-27**

1. In verse 26, Jesus uses the Greek word "deilos" for afraid. One of Strong's Concordance definitions for that term is "faithless." Where is there a place in your life right now where faith could cure your fear?

2. Where have you seen "wind and waves" obey Jesus in your own life or the lives of others? How does remembering those incidents strengthen your faith?

3. Find a Scripture that moves your spirit towards faith. Write it down, place it in a prominent spot, memorize it, and practice it. Use it, by speaking it out loud, whenever you sense the spirit of fear coming near. Write down any results.

## DIGGING DEEPER 17

**1 John 4:18**

1. How would you define perfect love?

2. In what way would perfect love drive out fear?

3. How do we allow ourselves to be punished by fear?

4. This verse reveals just how crucial renouncing fear is for anyone who wants to be made perfect in love. Compose a prayer centered around 1 John 4:18.

## DIGGING DEEPER 18

### Genesis 21:8-20

1. In verse 17, God tells Hagar not to be afraid. How does this story relate to defining the difference between facts and truth? Write out the facts of the circumstances surrounding Hagar and Ishmael. Then write out the truth concerning those circumstances.

2. Is there a circumstance in your life right now that has a tendency to provoke a feeling of fear in you? List the facts. Then list the truth.

# CHAPTER 5:

# GROUND BATTLES

• • • • • • • • • •

"Focus on the air battle"
Diane Gorsuch

IT WAS A SUNNY DAY IN LOUISVILLE, COLORADO. MY BEST friend's mom decided to take me out to lunch. I was living with her family during that season of life, doing youth ministry and working at Starbucks.

Diane inquired about my heart and life, and that passionate 19-year-old girl spilled out all the dramatic details of the things that surrounded her. I waited for Diane to respond with some opinion or instruction on how I should handle the situations I was facing. The words she spoke that day will be forever etched in my mind.

"Focus your efforts on the air battle, not the ground battle."

I was completely taken aback, having no real comprehension of what she meant. Diane patiently went on to explain to me all about the air battle of eternity that is constantly being waged all around us.

We are living on the ground of the world, but there is a whole other realm of existence, of which we can easily be unaware. As we live our lives on this ground, Satan will try his utmost to distract us from the things that really matter in eternity. He will use anything he can grasp to interfere with us gaining ground in the eternal battle, including those little things that drive us to fear. Those

• • • • • • • •

temporary things to which we apply all our energy so that our eyes are taken off the bigger, eternal picture.

How often do we view a person or circumstance as the enemy, instead of Satan? How often do we fret about things over which only God has control?

Satan will create drama to try to ensnare us into battling things out, in the flesh and on the ground. Fear will drive us to try and fix it all ourselves. Yet when we choose to fight on Satan's terms, we limit ourselves by not using the power with which God has equipped us. Fear stops us from fighting in faith. We become easily exhausted, anxiety becomes a constant companion, and the doom of defeat is always overhead.

Choosing to believe that we are who God says we are, however, allows us to overcome the accuser. The accuser will do whatever he can to tell us we're not good enough. The sneaky, contemptible scoundrel will even disguise himself in the cloak of God's law in order to convince us that we aren't enough. But with the power of the Holy Spirit and the law that gives life, we are more than conquerors. By faith, we know what the Holy Scriptures say. We know Who ultimately wins the war. No matter what ground Satan has now, it will be taken from him in the end. And when we choose to fight from the air with the authority that our great God has given to us and called us to use, we gain an eternal perspective. Then our impact will be great for the kingdom, the kingdom that will not fade away, but is for an eternity.

## DIGGING DEEPER 19

**Ephesians 6:12**

1. "We do not battle against flesh and blood." How does this Scripture clarify anything going on in your circumstances today?

2. Does thinking about the "heavenly realms" and the air battle blow your mind at all? How are the heavenly realms actually more real than the earthly realm?

3. Name a few instances when you've mistakenly struggled against flesh and blood, people, perceiving that they were the enemies?

## DIGGING DEEPER 20

**Ephesians 2:1-7**

1. Examine verses 2 and 3 and record your thoughts about them.

2. What did God do in verse 6? So technically, in the heavenly realms, where are we?

3. If we actually believe verse 6, then how easy is it to gain a perspective of the air battle?

4. What sight then, if we are sitting where God says we are sitting, might provoke us to live a life of gratitude?

## DIGGING DEEPER 21

### Colossians 1:13-23

1. Write down verses 13, 16, and 22. Underline "free from accusation" in verse 22.

2. Compose a prayer in response to these verses

## DIGGING DEEPER 22

### Daniel 10:7-14

1. In breaking down this small piece of Scripture, what can you gather about the spiritual realm?

2. The angel that spoke with Daniel referenced the "Prince of the Persian Kingdom," "the king of Persia," and "the prince of Greece." This leads us to believe that Satan has an order and system in which he conducts his business. It seems that he has put a certain presence in power over certain territories. When you think about the specific and certain rulers, authorities, powers of darkness, and forces of evil that might be in charge of your specific location, what is your first reaction? What is the appropriate response?

3. Is there any way you could believe that an angel might be sent in response to your prayer as it was to Daniel? Why?

4. How does this Scripture impact your view of the air battle?

# CHAPTER 6

# OTHER JARS

. . . . . . . . . .

"We rise by lifting others."
Hunting-loise

ONCE WE CATCH A GLIMPSE OF HOW GOD SEES US AND VALUES us, then we can see the value of others more clearly as well.

The spirit of fear wants to create intimidation. It wants you to be intimidated by the good things you see in others - or it wants you to feel the need to intimidate others with your own good things. When we are confident in our royal position, though, appreciating others in their unique positions becomes a joy. Valuing and even celebrating other broken, weak, but beautiful humans becomes part of our walk in life.

Judgment, bitterness, and jealousy can cease because we are confident in the power and love that resides in us - and in those around us.

I love how Steven Pressfield wrote, "Creative work is not a selfish act or a bid for attention on the part of the actor. It's a gift to the world and every being in it. Don't cheat us of your contribution. Give us what you've got." (*The War of Art*, page 165)

Seriously, how fantastic would it be if we contributed to the church everything we've got, and encouraged our brothers and sisters to do the same?!

. . . . . . . . .

Let's not concern ourselves about whether we "seem prideful" or if we "look humble" in the way we act. If we are walking with our God and being humbly obedient to His leading, then we can be confident in ourselves while also celebrating and granting grace to those around us.

A dear friend once told me that as she overcame this spirit of fear, she went from FEAR to FREEDOM to CONFIDENCE. Once we are free from fear, we have the freedom to be ourselves - broken out of the prison of what others think. We move forward in confidence because we know how God sees us and we believe what He has said. Onward we move in our identity, in our kingdoms, and on our battlefields, purposefully and successfully.

When we start to fill the piece of history we are intended to fill, it's easy to realize how much others need to fill their own piece. God's plan is to build his bride (the church) to be **one**, and as individuals, taking our proper place in the bride, we become aware of how valuable the person next to us truly is. We discover how very much we need her, or him, to build the church up.

As I grow, I find it easier and easier to replace bitterness with gratitude for my brothers and sisters in Christ. Christ in me continues to grow, and grace becomes more abundant. I can see that they, too, are seeking to do what's right. They are learning and walking a path similar to mine, filled with mountains and valleys, all leading to the ultimate prize.

Loving others with an agape love begins with loving who God made you to be. Believing that you have great value - seeing the clay pot you are as beautiful - is not vanity. It's maturity. It's not selfish to walk in your passions and dreams. In fact, the more you walk with God in these things, valuing who God made you to be, the less selfish you become. You see that your growth is God working in you, and you naturally give Him the glory. Seeing God in people around you also becomes easier, and you will find yourself growing a heart of gratitude towards them.

## DIGGING DEEPER 23

**Romans 12:3-8**

1. Pinpoint any places in your heart where you have a hard time embracing other members of the church.

2. Verse 5 states that we belong to each other. What feelings and thoughts does this provoke in you?

3. Evaluate how you are contributing to the body with your gifts. How you are encouraging others to do the same?

## DIGGING DEEPER 24

### Romans 14

1. This chapter is a lot to swallow. Take a moment to pray for someone who you feel has offended you. Ask God to help you become "unoffendable" and to empower you to both **feel** grace and **extend** grace to this person.

2. Record your thoughts on verse 15. Pray that God would make you aware of how your actions affect those around you.

3. Write out verse 19.

4. Create an action plan to apply this verse in at least two areas of your life.

## DIGGING DEEPER 25

### Jeremiah 29:11

1. Write out this verse.

2. Speak this verse out loud.

3. Speak this verse again, this time inserting the name of those people in your world who can be difficult.

4. After doing #3, have your feelings altered toward these people at all? Explain.

# PART II

# BE
# POWERFUL

· · · · · · · · · ·

We have been given a spirit of power.

## MISSION:

*Participate in the Spirit of Power by Balancing*
*Love and Discipline*

· · · · · · · · ·

# CHAPTER 1

# CLAIMING POWER

. . . . . . . . . .

"The kingdom of God is not a matter of talk but of power."
1 Corinthians 4:20

IN ORDER TO BE EFFECTIVE ROYALTY AND A SUCCESSFUL WAR-
rior, it is crucial not only to be aware of this power we've been given, but also to claim it and maintain it.

> "Then you will be made complete with all the fullness of life
> and power that comes from God.
>
> Now all glory to God, who is able, through his mighty power
> within us, to accomplish infinitely more than we might ask
> or think." (Ephesians 3:18-20)

When we feel overwhelmed, when our feet are slipping from underneath us, when we feel
attacked by that person or we can't wrap our head around this circumstance, or when the drone of
the everyday is just too much to bear - it's remembering who we are that will help us to actively live
in the spirit of power.

Practically speaking, how do we live powerfully in our daily ins and outs?

We can attempt to put forth immense effort to behave properly and thereby become powerful.
We can embrace our own work, in other words, and try to beat ourselves into an external appearance of what God is calling us to be.

. . . . . . . . .

But that's not the way. Amazingly enough, this spirit of power is a free gift that God bestows upon us. There is no earning it. We just adopt it. In fact, by attempting to earn it, we actually negate the gift of grace. When we accept Christ, we receive the spirit of power. There is no way to conjure it up inside of us. It's already there, if we've received Christ as our Lord. It's not our job to make ourselves like Christ. God makes us like Christ. All we are called to do is to claim and maintain His Spirit that is already within us.

To become powerful, we must submit to the process. When we have a mountain or a lion in front of us, we must fight the urge to run, to ignore it, or to shrink to the floor, throwing fits in defeat.

Be obedient to what God has called you to do, stand firm in it, and be patient. Allow God to use your circumstances, every moment, even the difficult ones for good. Allow His power to work in you, to strengthen and grow you.

God is faithful, and He will always show up and do His part. If we are acting powerless, or feeling powerless, then we are not doing *our* part. God has given us everything we need. If you are not powerful, then it's time to repent. Start believing that God is who He says He is, that God can do what He says He can do, that you are who God says you are, that you can do *all* things through Christ who strengthens you, and that the Word of God is alive and active in you.

Then start acting like an obedient child of the Heavenly Father, a faithful bride to the Holy Spirit, and a good friend to Jesus Christ your Lord.

## DIGGING DEEPER 1

### Luke 24:49, Acts 1:7 & 8, Acts 2:38 & 39

1. Have you become clothed with the "power from on high?" If so, when was it? Describe your experience(s).

2. When have you ever felt the call to stay where you were until given permission, power from Jesus, to proceed with what you were called to do?

## DIGGING DEEPER 2

### 2 Thessalonians 1:11

1. Pinpoint regular times when you tend to feel powerless in your daily life and write them down.

2. Write down this verse.

3. Record some of your "desires for goodness."

4. Create an action step prompted by faith that you can take when you are feeling powerless at any given moment. For example, choose a Scripture to memorize, a worship song to sing, a truth to declare, etc.

# DIGGING DEEPER 3

## 2 Corinthians 10:3-5

1. Contrast any times in your past when you've fought with weapons of this world versus weapons that have divine power.

2. How will you use this divine power to demolish arguments and pretensions that set themselves up against Christ?

# DIGGING DEEPER 4

## Ephesians 3:14-21

1. "That Christ may dwell in your hearts through faith." All the power that Paul the apostle is writing about here is only possible through faith. Write and then say out loud the following statements from Beth Moore's *Believing God* study:

   – I believe God is who He says He is.

   – I believe God can do what He says He can do.

   – I believe I am who God says I am.

   – I believe I can do all things through Christ who strengthens me.

   – I believe the Word of God is alive and active in me.

2. How would you measure your fullness of God? How do you increase your fullness?

3. How have you experienced God's power at work in you? Explain.

# CHAPTER 2

# MAINTAINING POWER

· · · · · · · · · ·

" God's part is to put forth power, our part is to put forth faith."
Andrew Bonar

THE FRUIT OF THE SPIRIT IS LOVE, JOY, PEACE, PATIENCE, kindness, goodness, faithfulness, gentleness, and self-control. If we want these fruits to be abundant in our lives, then our course of action must **not** be to "try." Trying to be more patient, faithful, good, or self-controlled can only get you so far. I'm sure I'm not the only one who has tried and failed to do these things more than I can count. The truth is we can't just **will** fruit to grow. Our desires and our feelings alone do not have power to do much good.

"God's righteousness doesn't grow from human anger." James 1:20 (The Message)

When a fruit tree is planted, it requires care in order to grow. It must be watered, it must soak in the sun, and the weeds around it must be uprooted so that the tree has space and an environment in which to expand. When these things happen, before you know it, the tree bears fruit. It just happens! Because the tree is well cared for, the fruit grows. We can't simply command the tree to produce fruit--rather, we nurture it, and the fruit naturally grows.

Sister! If your desire is to have a powerful spirit that produces abundant fruit, then tend to and maintain the Holy Spirit inside of you. **Your responsibility** is to tend to the Spirit, and **His responsibility** is to make you powerful.

· · · · · · · ·

Practically speaking, how do we tend to our spiritual "tree" to produce "fruit" and become more powerful in our daily lives?

- Pray--nurture your spirit by allowing yourself time in His presence. Consistently acknowledge and interact with Him throughout your day.

- Learn the Bible--meditate on and soak in Scriptures, quenching yourself with living water. Read it regularly, listen to it, and post it around your living spaces where you'll see it.

- Worship--bask in thankfulness to the Son, rejuvenating your mind and heart.

- Fellowship--feed your spirit with laughter and tears and camaraderie of people who are like-minded. This includes teachings from mentors as well as encouragement from friends and family.

Renewing our minds is the best way to spot the lies and maintain our spirit of power. As we fill our minds with the truth, we will easily spot and dismiss the lies that come our way. We must dismiss false thoughts with the all-surpassing power and authority God has given us, because those thoughts can be quite persistent.

As this spirit of power grows in you, you will be more able to exercise your authority over Satan, your past, your circumstances, and your flesh.

## DIGGING DEEPER 5
........................................................

### Psalm 1:2 & 3

1. How can you be like a tree that yields fruit in season and whose leaf does not wither?

2. Notice that this tree yields its fruit in season; it's not expected to yield fruit all year long, but it goes through the appropriate seasons. Spring, summer, fall, and winter pass, and the tree only yields when the time comes for it to yield. Although the living water is a constant source of nourishment, fruit might not be visible until the right season. Can you trust that fruit is being grown inside of you even in a wintery season?

3. Consider someone you might know who always prospers, even in difficult times. Write down their names and some thoughts about the way they prosper.

## DIGGING DEEPER 6

........................................................

### Jeremiah 17:5-10

1. Have you ever found yourself drawing strength from mere flesh? Maybe felt like a bush in the wastelands? Explain.

2. Have you ever noticed yourself focusing more on the bad and unable to see where you're actually prospering and being blessed? Maybe there have been times you've chosen to dwell in a parched place by yourself. Write down any confessions, and take time to repent if you need to. If not, take a moment to prayerfully consider this concept. Write out anything that is revealed to you.

3. "But blessed is the one who trusts in the Lord, whose confidence is in Him." It seems that we can choose to be parched, or we can choose to be blessed. What are you choosing today? How can we choose to be blessed?

4. As you examine verses 9-10, what sort of peace do you receive knowing that you don't need to understand those around you and that only the Lord is in charge of dispatching rewards and consequences? Prayerfully write out a response to these verses.

5. Examine whether there are any spots of your spirit that need some Son. What are the things in your mind or heart that have been hiding in the dark, that need to come into the light to be healed? Write about any sin that needs to be confessed and exposed.

6. Find someone in whom you can confide about those areas and ask them to hold you accountable.

## DIGGING DEEPER 7

........................................................

### Galatians 5:22-26

1. For what reason would one want to crucify the flesh with its passions and desires?

2. How does "keep in step with the spirit" line up with the concept of "maintain your power"?

3. Practically speaking, how does one not become conceited, and not provoke or envy others?

4. Does your answer to the previous question stir any kind of compassion in you for others who you witness displaying those characteristics?

5. What fruit would you like to see become more prominent in you?

........

6. Write out a prayer asking that God would reveal what you can do to help this fruit grow in you. What are the weeds (bad habits or thoughts patterns) that you need to remove because they are hindering the fruit's growth?

CHAPTER 3:

# THE ENEMY

• • • • • • • • • •

"The enemy is not fighting you because you are weak.
He's fighting you because you're strong."
Lancelearning.biz

IN MATTHEW 13, JESUS TALKS ABOUT A FARMER WHO PLANTS GOOD SEED, but then an enemy comes in the night to spread bad seed in his fields. The farmer instructs the harvesters to let all the seed grow together and then, come harvest, separate the good wheat from the weeds. In His explanation of this story, Jesus states, "The enemy who sows is the devil. The harvest is the end of the age, and the harvesters are the angels." (*Matthew 13:39*)

Here we are with good seed in us, doing our best to cultivate it. But we are also living among bad seed planted by the devil. The biggest way the weeds can choke us out as we wait for harvest (redemption) is to make us forget--or worse, not believe--that we are who God says we are.

"Be alert and of sober mind. Your enemy the
devil prowls around like a roaring lion looking
for someone to devour," says 1 Peter 5:8.

In his book *Spiritual Warfare*, Dr. David Jeremiah references Naturalist Craig Child sharing about a time he was hiking and came across a lion. This man knew that if he kept walking, ignoring the lion, then it would pounce on him. He also knew he couldn't outrun this creature. So instead, he

• • • • • • • •

stood his ground and looked this lion straight in the eye. Eventually, the lion left. He walked away from the man--a mere human.

> "Put on the full armor of God so that you can take your stand against the devil's schemes...when the day of evil comes, you may be able to stand your ground, and after you have done everything to stand." (Ephesians 6:10, 11, 13)

> "Submit yourselves, then, to God, resist the devil and he will flee from you."

> (James 4:7)

One of my heroes, Havilah Cunnington, preaches that although the devil is a kleptomaniac--coming to steal and kill and destroy--oftentimes he doesn't even need to steal from us. Too often, we willingly hand him our power without even resisting. One little lie and we'll agree with him, allowing him to put a shackle on us.

Satan has no power over you unless you give it to him. Don't! Whatever part of you he might have taken from you, take it back. We have authority to trample on snakes and scorpions and to overcome all the power of the enemy. Let's use it.

## DIGGING DEEPER 8
..............................................

### John 10:10

1. Can you pinpoint any times when the "thief" has stolen from you? Write about a time Satan got what was rightfully yours.

2. How would you define "life to the full"?

## DIGGING DEEPER 9
..............................................

### 1Peter 5:8-11

1. Write about a time when you encountered a "lion" situation in your life and how you handled it. Did you ignore it, run from it, or stand your ground? Examine the outcome.

2. How does knowing that your family of believers is also undergoing suffering help you to "stand"?

## DIGGING DEEPER 10

**James 4:7**

1. Resisting the Devil comes only after submission to God. Have you tried to resist the Devil lately but he hasn't fled? Perhaps there is an area in your life that isn't completely submitted to God. Prayerfully write out your response.

2. How does full submission to God empower you to resist the Devil? Have you ever been so immersed in Him that when anything dark or sinful came near, it was obvious and easy to resist? "The light shines in the darkness and the darkness has not overcome it." (John 1:5)

## DIGGING DEEPER 11

**Romans 16:20**

1. Under whose feet will Satan be crushed?

2. Compose a prayer of praise. Rejoice and thank God for the power He has given you over Satan, and ask Him to grow that power in you. Pray that you will be one who cannot be deceived.

CHAPTER 4:

# ATTITUDE & CIRCUMSTANCE

• • • • • • • • •

"God often showcases his power on the stage of human weakness."

Andy Stanley

MY DAD USED TO TELL ME TO "FIX YOUR ATTITUDE." ALTHOUGH that is great instruction, when we are told such things, we aren't really in a mindset to embrace the exhortation. Yet when we allow circumstances and emotions to have power over us, it is reflected-in our attitudes.

Attitude can be defined as "a way of thinking that affects a person's behavior". Changing our attitude means changing the way we think, so it's not something that we can change easily. However, it is absolutely important that we take the time to arrest our thoughts and attitudes and align them with the Truth. The Bible says that we do have complete power over this.

No matter what is physically happening in our body or our surroundings, we've been given power to have a spirit that is successful and strong! We are by no means compelled to allow our circumstances to have power over our attitudes.

Our to-do lists are big, but those lists do not have the power to control how we handle them, unless we allow lists to take our power. If our lists control us, then we are allowing fear, anxiety, or

• • • • • • • • •

pride access to our hearts. This mentality also affects our moods and our responses to those around us.

Another critical aspect is our feelings. Emotions are good, and we certainly should allow our emotions to have some healthy influence over our behavior and our choices. **But sister**, don't be afraid to lovingly take hold of your emotions and say, "Thank you very much, emotions, for your opinions. I will now let my sound mind make the decisions."

Your Highness - do not give your power over to your emotions.

Warrior - do not allow your emotions to have power over you.

Sometimes the battles that come our way are in our bodies. If you have dealt with chronic pain, depression, any kind of disease, or even grief, then you know that living in a spirit of power might feel impossible. "With man this is impossible, but with God all things are possible." (Matthew 19:26)

I struggle with anxiety at times. But I've learned that even when my body is affected by it, my spirit doesn't need to suffer from it.

One time I was on the floor in the middle of an anxiety attack, sobbing, and yet still certain that I possessed a peace that surpassed understanding that was guarding my heart and mind. I remembered what it says in Philippians 4:6 & 7: "Be anxious for nothing, but in all things by prayer and petition, with thanksgiving, present your requests to God. <u>And the peace of God, which transcends understanding will guard your hearts and minds in Christ Jesus.</u>"

Fear spoke then, pointing out the whole **be anxious for nothing** part of the verse, and said "You're not good enough--you aren't being obedient in this area--so you can't have peace."

Then the practice of renewing my mind came into play, even in the midst of a physical breakdown. I know my body is an earthly tent and can only handle so much. If it shuts down or trembles in pain, I can still say, "I know that I am royalty, co-heir to the throne. I know that my heart and mind are anchored on Christ. Even though my body is crumpled and crying on the ground, my spirit stands firm and my peace is secure. I'm good enough because Christ has covered me, and God says I'm good enough. Satan, be gone. Fear, you are dismissed. Doubt, go away in the name of Jesus! I'm going to choose to rest my body and lay at my Father's feet. He will restore me, and then my body will go back to the work that God has prepared for me. In this moment, weak and weepy, I will worship Him and bring Him glory."

Now, perhaps I wasn't quite so eloquent in the moment. But ramblings filled with truth are just as powerful as truth spoken articulately. Romans 8:27 & 28 says that the Spirit Himself intercedes on our behalf:

"In the same way the Spirit helps us in our weakness.
We do not know what we ought to pray for, but the
Spirit himself intercedes for us through wordless
groans. And he who searches our hearts knows the
mind of the Spirit, because the Spirit intercedes for
God's people in accordance with the will of God."

Sisters, don't ever hesitate to pray, even when you don't know what to say. The Spirit will be more eloquent and articulate than any human could ever be.

When we are weak, it gives God the opportunity to be strong for us; even in our broken bodies and weak efforts, the spirit of power endures and stands. When the spirit of power is claimed and maintained in us, we will not be defeated, even in our weakest moments.

## DIGGING DEEPER 12

### Philippians 4:4-9

1. Write out verse 8.

2. If we were obedient to this and had these kinds of thoughts, how would that reflect in our attitudes?

3. Verse 5 says to let your gentleness be evident to all, following right after instructions to rejoice. Have you found it easier to be gentle while experiencing joy? Record any thoughts you have regarding this.

4. Have you experienced an unexplainable peace after choosing to have an attitude of gratitude? Write down any testimony you have regarding this. Compose a prayer of thanksgiving surrounding the circumstances you're in right now. Take note of how it affects your peace

## DIGGING DEEPER 13

### 2 Corinthians 12:9-10

1. In what areas are you feeling particularly weak right now?

2. Compose a prayer praising God for His grace and asking Him to make His power perfect in those places. Praise Him that because of His grace, we can accept our weaknesses without shame.

3. Make an effort to choose delight in whatever difficulties come your way. Write down your difficulties on a piece of paper and put it in a prominent spot. Pray for the Spirit to empower you with joy in the midst of it all. Revisit this paper a week later and record your results. Whether it was a success or failure, God's grace is enough. You can celebrate that your weakness did not defeat you!

## DIGGING DEEPER 14

**Romans 8:26 & 27**

1. "The Spirit helps us in our weakness. We do not know what we ought to pray..." When you think about where you're weak, is prayer your first thought? It makes sense that we might be weak in any given area because we haven't prayed. Compose a prayer of thanksgiving surrounding these verses.

2. I get such delight from the concept that the Spirit translates my muttered prayers into something that lines up "according to His will." Write out a confession of a time when you prayed selfish prayers, knowing that what you were asking actually went against what you knew about God's character. How reassuring is it to know that the Spirit was translating it "according to the will of God" as He interceded?

3. Has there ever been an instance that you felt so lost for words in prayer, but were able to fellowship with the Spirit with the knowledge that He was searching your heart and interceding on your behalf? If you have any testimony about God turning your prayers into something beautiful, write it out and share it with someone.

# CHAPTER 5:

# POWER OVER THE PAST

"Your past does not define you. It prepares you."
Unknown

WE'VE BEEN GIVEN A SPIRIT OF POWER THAT CLAIMS ALL OF our past for God's glory. When things from our past resurface to haunt or shake us, we have power over how that affects us.

In other words, we can take our bad memories and put them in a new frame, a frame that highlights the faithfulness and goodness and deliverance of God.

God doesn't even remember the sin in our past. He forgets, but He allows us to remember so that our present and our future will be protected. Our past may want to condemn us and keep us sitting still in shame instead of moving forward. But remember this: "There is no condemnation for those that are in Christ Jesus." (Romans 8:1) So we remember our past only in order to pave the way for success, not condemnation.

Only when we stop allowing our past to empower our behavior negatively can we live in victory. This victory allows past failures to motivate our present obedience. When we recall that time we failed, we don't want it to happen again. Therefore, we choose obedience in this moment, hoping for a better outcome.

Maintaining power over our past gives God the center stage, revealing that His hand is always upon us. This means taking those memories before the throne and asking God to reveal Himself in them. It means when that feeling comes in the pit of your stomach, as memories prance tauntingly across your thoughts, you capture those thoughts and speak truth over them, while casting them before an almighty God who is abounding in grace.

In referring to "the past", I've been talking about those young years when you were quite foolish, those memories of the awful things you did and the awful things done to you.

But this is also about yesterday and this morning and a few minutes ago.

Don't hand your power to the past. We absolutely have power over how we view the past, while still allowing it to shape our present and future.

Jesus Christ has made the ultimate sacrifice. You don't need to sacrifice your present peace and joy for anything that's happened in the past. Don't let that accuser, Satan, make you believe anything different.

## DIGGING DEEPER 15

### Isaiah 43:18 & 19

1. Are there specific bad memories that you have a hard time forgetting, or at least not dwelling on? Write down the effect they have on you.

2. Examine your life in this moment and record the new things you see God bringing forth. What are the ways He is making for you in the wilderness and where are the streams in the wasteland?

## DIGGING DEEPER 16

### Hebrews 10:17 & 18

1. Do you really think God forgets your sins and lawless acts? Explain.

2. How can you use the memories you have of your sinful and lawless acts to your advantage?

3. Can you see any places in your life where you've sacrificed good things in order to try to "earn" God's forgiveness instead of accepting Christ's sacrifice? Do you think you will be able to shift your mentality so that you can rest in the truth of verse 18?

## DIGGING DEEPER 17

**Romans 8:1 & 2**

1. Write down and memorize this Scripture.

2. Say it out loud.

3. Keep this verse in your "pocket" and use it whenever you are tempted to feel condemnation or shame.

## DIGGING DEEPER 18

**Romans 8:28-30**

1. For whom do all things work together for the good? Is this promise for everyone?

2. It has been said that we should look at life as though everything that happens to us is "on the way," instead of "in the way." We need to view everything we encounter in life as something that God is using to conform us to the image of His Son. Today, what is on the way to making you be conformed to the image of Christ?

3. You are predestined to be in relationship with the Trinity. What else has He done for you? (v.30)

4. You will not miss the call. When He calls you, you will hear Him. Have you heard God's call on your life?

5. In turn, Christ will justify you, at once and completely. At the end of time, He will justify your every action and word. Picture yourself being confronted with all the decisions you made in life and having Christ before you, justifying each and every thought, word, and action. Write a prayer in response.

6. What does it mean to you to be glorified?

# DIGGING DEEPER 19

### Romans 8:33 & 34

1. Pinpoint times that you "bring charge" against yourself regarding your past. Do you have people in your life who tend to stir up past things to charge against you? Do you ever have an evil spirit that taunts you, charging you with your misdeeds? Explain.

2. Prayerfully ask God to make you aware of when you start to agree with these self-condemning thoughts or feelings. Ask the Spirit to remind you that it is God who justifies and that Christ Jesus who died, and was raised, is sitting at the throne interceding for you. Write out your prayer.

3. Are there any people in your world who you may need to stop condemning? Ask God to heal your wounds and empower you to allow the Almighty God to justify that person, His chosen one. Trust that He will make it right, God will disperse punishment as He sees fit. Write down your prayers and thoughts.

# CHAPTER 6

# OBEDIENCE

• • • • • • • • •

"No one doth safely rule but he that hath learned gladly to obey."
Thomas a Kempis

ONE DAY, AS I WAS *TRYING* TO LOAD ALL FOUR OF MY LITTLE boys into our SUV for an outing, my second son took his sweet time looking through our yard instead of proceeding to the truck.

He finally made it over to where his frustrated mother was calling him and held up his little fist, which was overflowing with dandelions. He was quite proud of himself as he handed them to me. He lovingly said, "Here, Mom, I picked you some flowers!"

I responded, "Yes, son, I see. But I need you to show me you love me by being obedient."

*Bam.* Internally, I felt the Spirit's prodding asking, "Christine, are you handing the Lord weeds instead of coming when He calls? Good intentions are great, but obedience is better than sacrifice."

Let us be women who are completely obedient. Oswald Chambers says this: "A child's life is normally obedient, until he chooses disobedience. But as soon as he chooses to disobey, an inherent inner conflict is produced. On the spiritual level, inner conflict is the warning of the Spirit of God. When he warns us in this way, we must stop at once and be renewed in the spirit of our mind to discern God's will."

This description reminds me of times when I warn one of my boys not to continue doing something once, maybe twice, and then, if they have chosen to still disobey me, I begin moving towards

• • • • • • • •

them to create a consequence. They already *know* to respond right away and to stop immediately when I speak to them, yet they had chosen disobedience.

This is a reflection of how we must behave with our Lord. Let's have sensitive ears to any warnings our Lord may give us at any given moment.

We cannot claim God's promises with a "kinda". We mustn't think that if we obey half way, we can receive all the rewards He has for us.

My children give me halfhearted obedience all the time. If I tell my son to put specific shoes on and go outside, and he proceeds to pick a different set of shoes and take 30 minutes to move his way out the door while goofing around and being distracted, has he been obedient? Kinda. He has also been DISobedient.

So if the Spirit tells you "don't buy that" by giving you a lack of peace, and you merely wait until you have more spending money to do so, you can't claim to have obeyed because you didn't buy it *right then.*

If He says "don't talk about that" and then you share it with "only" a few trusting ears… that is disobedience.

In Genesis, God asked Abraham to sacrifice his only son, and Abraham was obedient, all the way to the point that God stopped him. Did God really want Abraham to kill his son as a sacrifice? No. He wanted Abraham's obedience. Genesis 22:16 says, "I swear by myself, declares the Lord, that because you have done this, and not withheld your son, your only son, I will surely bless you…"

God is not asking you to literally sacrifice your son. Maybe He's asking you to give a bit of your time to church, or to another place of service. Perhaps He's asking you to choose some Scripture instead of the snooze button in the morning--or maybe to humble yourself and confess, or confront someone instead of ignoring conflict.

Maybe God is asking you to climb that mountain instead of going around it. Do it. Go all in and give Him your complete obedience. You will not be sorry. Don't take the easy route and go around. Sure, you might end up in the same place as those who've climbed, but there is no victory in that journey, no character muscle built, and the growth is minimal.

Climbing the mountain is hard, it burns, and you might really need to strain. But the view is outlandishly better, and the victory and taste of accomplishment, the air up there, and the ride down are all worth it.

However, there is no way we can pursue this path of obedience without the power of the Holy Spirit in us.

God will bless us. It's his nature. He is a good Father, who takes care of His daughters, even if we choose to be disobedient. But to be a successful Royal Warrior, we must be fully obedient and not halfhearted.

When my children are fellowshipping with me, it is easy for them to know my will. If they want something, they can look my way and recognize either an approving nod or a *don't you dare* glare. Let us be in the Lord's presence and look His way as we do what's before us. Then we can go forth in power, claiming all that God has for us, swimming in His abundant fruit and blessings.

## DIGGING DEEPER 20

**James 1:2-7**

1. Define a time when it was hard to be faithful while you faced trials. According to this Scripture, why should we be faithful?

2. Who does God give generously to?

3. Who can't expect to receive anything from the Lord?

4. How can you rest assured that you will receive from the Lord?

## DIGGING DEEPER 21

**Psalm 37**

1. List all the promises from God in this Scripture and what they are "contingent" on. EXAMPLE: <u>He will give you the desires of your heart</u> - **Delight in the Lord.**

## DIGGING DEEPER 22

**Hebrews 11:6**

1. Who does God reward?

2. Is it possible to be disobedient while earnestly seeking God? Explain.

3. What is a main requirement to please God?

4. Define the faith in your life that pleases God.

# DIGGING DEEPER 23

## Galatians 5:16-18

1. Have you experienced a time when you were so saturated with the Spirit's presence that it was very easy to NOT gratify your flesh? If not, do you believe this kind of thing is possible?

2. Examine how to "walk by the Spirit." Record your ponderings and discoveries.

3. When was the last time you really felt the conflict between your flesh and the Spirit within you?

4. How have you handled this conflict in the past? Make a plan for future conflicts.

5. Prayerfully consider your level of obedience this last year, last week, and today. Respond with repentance and celebration, for God's grace is to be glorified through both your failures and success!

6. Compose a prayer asking the Spirit to empower you to walk with Him in obedience--and freedom.

## CHAPTER 7:

# THE KINGDOM

. . . . . . . . . .

"Nothing will ever change while you point the finger of blame.
Out of responsibility come possibility."
Lisa Villa Prosen

*AS THE WEIGHT OF HER BURDENS GREW SHE SIGHED DEEPLY. HER RESPON-sibilities were many, and her territory was large.*

*She had known that when she came of age, the land and power she received would require much of her. She just hadn't expected it to be so… hard.*

*Listening to the reports being given to her, she glanced out the castle window and noticed that most of her fields were dry and shriveled, while just a few were well-watered and fruitful.*

*The source bearing news to her was communicating that one corner of her territory was under attack from a neighboring city and therefore required more of her resources. There were also reports that the east wall might have been compromised and was in need of reinforcement, while on the north end, there was word that thieves were spotted crossing into her territory. And then there was news of vandalism to the south, bringing extra weight to her already weary heart, mind, and body.*

*Once she was alone, the realization of it all came crashing around her. Crumbling to the floor in despair, her large, heavy skirts became her cushion as she wept. Relief of her tears finally settled over her and she shifted her weight rising to a kneeling position. Throwing off every pressure coming at her, urging her to hurry out and take charge of her business, she committed to take as much time as needed in quiet.*

. . . . . . . . .

*Closing her eyes, she entered the heavenly throne room and prayed. Relaxing in her Lord's arms in the moment and receiving a fresh wind of strength that seemed to spread through her. Possibly dosing off a bit, the desire to stay in this place forever burned in her heart, yet eventually, there was a prod from the Holy Spirit that said it was time.*

*She rose, straightened her hair, and freshened her face with renewed confidence. Knowing now what's needing to be done.*

*And she determined that she would kneel again soon. She would rest with her Lord, being renewed by the Spirit before she reached this point again.*

*Enlivened to the work before her, she moved swiftly to take control of her territory and reinforce her borders. Refusing to be a victim.*

This scene is one I think any woman can relate to.

With adulthood comes responsibility. God has given us all a load to bear as we journey in this life, and He's given us a territory to care for. We will call this territory our kingdom.

God has gifted each of us with our individual kingdom, in which we conduct both our business and our battles. In our kingdom, we are held responsible for our emotions, attitudes, and decisions. Nobody else is powerful enough to control any of these; we own them.

Maintaining our power within our own kingdoms is crucial to our success in the spiritual realm. If we extend ourselves too much by seeking to gain greater territory, yet haven't taken care of what we already have, for example, we will end up weary and broken and dry. Whatever good works God has ordained for us, we are responsible to be good stewards of them. If you want to thrive spiritually, then make sure that you attend to the business on your territory with the best of your ability, as worship unto the Lord.

We will encounter different battles within our kingdom as the seasons of our lives change. In each season, we need to prayerfully determine which battles are worth fighting. Sometimes we don't have a choice, when circumstances and divine providence bring them our way. But many times, we must be intentional in choosing which battles to engage in.

Yes, we can do all things through Christ, but God has not called us to do **all** things.

We will be called to do things that are outside our comfort zone - new things or things we've failed at before - and God will give us everything we need to overcome and do those things. Through Christ, everything is possible!

But God can use you without abusing you. He doesn't need to drain all your strength and energy to use you. God has called us to sacrifice our selfishness, not our sanity. He has specific things in mind for you, but not all things.

Our culture likes to communicate that we can and should do everything. This, however, is not the way Jesus led us.

Since our main responsibilities in our kingdoms include our emotions, attitudes, and decisions, it's critical that we tend to ourselves first. Without a healthy heart and mind, these three things are at risk of being compromised.

Jesus honored the Sabbath, and He took time alone with His Father. This was crucial to His human body as He had to manage his emotions, attitudes, and decisions as a human. *God the Father* even rested during creation. It is important that we examine how the Lord lived as we seek to follow Him and be like Jesus.

We will also see that Jesus never took on the responsibilities of anyone else's kingdoms.

You are not responsible for other people's actions. God has given you a responsibility to honor Him and to honor those people around you. But you are not responsible for the people around you. You have **not** been given the power to control anyone else's emotions, attitudes, or decisions. Again, you are responsible *to* others, not *for* others. Refuse to take on the anxiety of responsibilities that aren't yours!

In addition, no one ever dictated Jesus' responses; instead, He chose all of His own reactions and replies with a sound mind.

When we let others dictate our responses--what we feel and how we act--we have handed our power over to them, yet our God has graced us with the power over ourselves. Knowing what our responsibilities are allows us to keep our mind and power in the right place.

Own your **own** stuff. No one else is responsible for the decisions you make and the responses you choose to give.

Note: While each adult has their own territory, small children are a different matter. Their little kingdoms that hold their emotions, attitudes, and decisions are on your property as a parent. You most definitely should have power over how they handle their responsibilities. And as a parent or supervisor of these young ones, you must be on guard. Their untrained flesh will most assuredly try to steal your power and overthrow your rule!

## DIGGING DEEPER 24

**Matthew 25:14-29**

1. In your journal, use a page to draw a square representing your kingdom. Along the border of your territory, write "my emotions, my attitudes, my decisions."

2. In verse 24, we see the servant **assuming** that his master is a "hard man" who harvests and gathers what is not his. This man allowed fear to take over to the point where he actually blamed his bad choice on the master. Write down choices you've made in the past where you've tended to hold someone else responsible. (Take your time. While doing this exercise, don't forget that there is no condemnation under Christ! )

3. Imagine the day that you are before the Lord, presenting Him with the gifts He had you steward, and then being able to see all the fruit of your labor. Write a prayerful response to this thought.

## DIGGING DEEPER 25

**Ephesians 2:10**

1. Describe an instance where you may have thought that you "are God's handiwork, created in Christ Jesus to do (**ALL**) good works."

2. On the page next to your kingdom, write down all the works you are doing right now. For example, the business you conduct on a daily/weekly/monthly basis, the battles you are fighting, the jobs you are engaged in, etc.

3. Split your kingdom into two sections. Divide the list you created in question 2 into two categories. On one side, write the battles you **need** to fight (i.e. being a good mother, wife, employee), and on the other side write the battles you are **choosing** to fight, but that perhaps aren't required responsibilities.

4. Evaluate all the things in your kingdom and prayerfully determine if they are "good things" or "God things." Before deciding to commit to anything, first determine:

   – Is this a bad thing, good thing, or a God thing?

   – Do I have room in my kingdom for this?

(God things are a must, while good things are completely admissible <u>if</u> there is room in your kingdom.)

## DIGGING DEEPER 26

**2 Corinthians 11:18-20, Matthew 5:38-42**

1. Can't you just sense Paul's sarcasm here?! How might one feel as though they were strong to put up with being enslaved, exploited, taken advantage of, or slapped in the face?

2. How does this verse compare to Matthew 5:38-42? Jesus implies that we are to willingly take the abuse, while Paul implies we're wrong to do so. Describe how the context of these verses are different and how they, in fact, do not contradict each other.

3. How does having your power in place over your emotions, attitudes, and decisions ensure that you are not enslaved, exploited, taken advantage of, or slapped as Paul describes?

## DIGGING DEEPER 27

**Revelations 3:20**

1. How does this reflect the Lord respecting the territory He's given us?

2. Write out a commitment to make an effort to honor others' territory the way our God honors them.

3. The Lord says He will come and dine with us in rich, intimate fellowship. (Christine J. version) This is a very good thing! Can you pinpoint a time when you offered to give a very good thing to someone you cared for and they did not take you up on it? Were you able to respect their "no" answer, or did you feel the need to proceed with your "gift-giving", despite the response they gave you?

## DIGGING DEEPER 28

**Mark 10:17-22**

1. We see here how Jesus defines a boundary line for His territory. What did He tell the man he had to do in order to receive treasure in heaven from Jesus?

2. Jesus allowed the man to make his choice without compromising His boundary line, while also respecting the man's kingdom. He did not change His statement once He saw how the man responded, there was no running after the ruler begging him to comply. Reflect on your

recent interactions with those around you. Compose a prayer asking God to grow this same mindset in you.

3. How did Jesus feel about the ruler (vs 21)? How do his actions, or lack thereof, reflect real love?

CHAPTER 8:

# BOUNDARY LINES AND BATTLEFIELDS

. . . . . . . . .

*"Love is a battlefield"*
Pat Bentatar

"HEARTACHE TO HEARTACHE WE STAND!" THAT PAT BENATAR song is so fun, and it actually holds some big truth. God has called us to stand in the midst of heartache!

Although Jesus maintained boundaries, He also willingly allowed people into His sphere who were going to betray Him (such as Judas, Peter, and you & me). We know we are called to be vulnerable and to love with a 1 Corinthians 13 love, but how do we bear all things, while still guarding our hearts?

Stay in tune with the Holy Spirit, walk with Jesus, and seek the Father for guidance.

There is no fine print here. It is crucial that we seek God's counsel **before** we draw or extend the boundary lines of our kingdom--for example, before we unite with another person in the covenant of marriage, joining large parts of our territory with them, and then as our children grow and their territory extends beyond our own. Additionally, we must consider this whenever we work in any team. We must define the boundary lines according to the counsel of the One who will give us the eternal perspective.

. . . . . . . . .

I've found that the pattern in our culture is for people to shirk their responsibilities and reach instead for anyone who is willing to come and fight the battles in their kingdom for them. As a result, some compassionate people might find themselves fighting so many battles on other people's property, that their own heart and their own kingdom is left un-maintained. These people then reach out for help, bringing some other compassionate person into their kingdom to take care of their battles, since they are so busy with other people's. And on it goes. So many people in our generation are placing their responsibilities on others.

Now it's true that we are called to do the hard stuff together. But we must also maintain our own territory **and** respect others' property.

When we go onto a battlefield in someone else's kingdom without God calling us to do so, we steal from that person the victories that their struggles bring. Not only that, this leaves our own kingdom, our own battlefields, unattended and vulnerable.

Sometimes people might ask us take over some business in their kingdom when they get overwhelmed, or perhaps we see someone struggling in a battle and we want to save them. In such cases, we may lend a hand if both our hands aren't already engaged in the responsibilities and battles happening in our own kingdom. But I know that there have been times when I've taken on things that I had no business putting my hands to. If you look around, you might also find yourself on a battlefield or in a kingdom that is not your own.

We also can give up our power by allowing or even asking someone to come into our kingdom to fight for us without that request being ordained by God. Sometimes we look to others for help when really we should be seeking the Holy Spirit. Psalm 60:11 states that human help is worthless. Sometimes God is doing something bigger in our life than what we or any other human can see. One term for this is sanctification.

Often God **will** give us aid in the form a person. I can't even count the number of times when I've known people were sent straight from my Father to give me aid! Yet we must be diligent to not reach out and bring or allow someone onto our battlefield **without** the anointing of God.

Galatians 6 is rich with instruction on this topic. Verse 5 states "for each one should carry their own load." This Greek word for "load" is phortion. It is the same word used in Matthew 11:30 when Jesus said "my yoke is easy and my _burden_ is light."

This is the daily toil, the normal business, the works for which we are responsible in our territory, our kingdom.

Yet we all have those times when things come across our territory that demand everything we've got. Sometimes raging battles spring up, and it is crucial that we ask for help. A few verses above Galatians 6:5, where it tells us to carry our own load, we find verse 2, which states, "Carry each other's burdens, and in this way you will fulfill the law of Christ."

This word "burden" in verse 2 is <u>baros,</u> which refers to the notion of going down. This is a trouble that is just too heavy. It's the same word used in Acts 15:28, when Paul gives only four guidelines to new believers so as to not "burden" them with requirements.

Therefore, when we see a neighbor who is feeling weak from the weight of the burden upon them, struggling with the battles in their territory - we step in to fulfill the law of Christ: "We who are strong ought to bear with the failings of the weak and not to please ourselves, each of us should please our neighbors for their good to build them up." (Romans 15:1-2)

So sister, let's let God do His thing, and get out of the way by faithfully doing our part. God will show us when we should extend a hand to help. When we show up and do our part, and allow Him to do the rest, there is no way we can lose!

## DIGGING DEEPER 29

### Proverbs 4:23

1. Define "guard your heart" in your own words.

2. What does it look like to be authentic and vulnerable, while still guarding your heart?

3. How does guarding your heart play a part in being responsible for your kingdom?

## DIGGING DEEPER 30

### Matthew 7:6

1. Describe an experience you've had when you were torn to pieces after sharing a precious pearl of yourself.

2. How can creating a discerning guard around your heart help you to be obedient to this proverb?

3. Are there people in your life with whom you can share the pearls that God has given you without any fear of it being trampled on by them? Write out their names.

4. Compose a prayer asking God to bestow on you good discernment regarding what and with whom you share.

## DIGGING DEEPER 31

........................................................

**Proverbs 25:28**

1. Explain one or two instances where your lack of self-control resulted in what seemed like an invasion.

2. Take a moment to envision yourself as a kingdom. Draw a sketch of your kingdom. Draw the different districts and label them. Get creative, maybe adding parks, ponds, a river, etc. Then take a moment to draw a wall around your city. Take note where the wall, your discipline, is weaker.

3. Write a prayer of thanksgiving for the "kingdom" that God has blessed you with and petition the Spirit to strengthen your wall - to work in you the discipline needed to guard your heart. Ask Him to work in you a discernment that loves and communicates Christ to everyone around you.

## DIGGING DEEPER 32

........................................................

**John 21:15-22**

1. The Lord challenges Peter to meet his failure of denying Jesus three times by declaring his love three times, and then look forward at what's to be done now. What are the failures in your past that need to be faced? Perhaps they need your love for God and your readiness to move on declared over them? Record your response.

2. In what ways is God asking you to feed His sheep? Define what obedience to this might look like in your kingdom.

3. Where have you found yourself looking over at another person's kingdom and asking God, "What about them?"

4. Allow your heart to hear God say, "**YOU** must follow me." Then determine to put your focus on where He's leading you - not where He's leading others. Write a prayerful response.

## DIGGING DEEPER 33

........................................................

**John 18:8-11**

1. Why did Peter have a sword and why did he feel the need to fight to free Jesus? (Luke 22:36-38)

........

2. How can this Scripture be applied to the concept of boundary lines and battlefields that we are learning about?

3. Pinpoint a time where you may have jumped the gun, like Peter, thinking you needed to defend or fight for someone, when really, they needed to "drink the cup" the Father had given them.

# PART III

# Intimately Entwined with the Trinity

· · · · · · · · ·

We have been given a Spirit of Love

## THE MISSION:

*Embrace the Royal Title by Being Entwined with the Trinity.*

· · · · · · · ·

# CHAPTER I

# AGAPE

· . . . . . . . · ·

"So we have come to know and to believe the love that God
has for us. God is love, and whoever abides in love, abides in
God, and God in them."

1 John 4:16

"AGAPE" IS A TERM USED ABUNDANTLY THROUGHOUT THE
Scriptures, a total of 259 times in the New Testament. "Agape" is the Greek word that Scripture uses
in the effort to encapsulate the love of God in one utterance.

I admit: I am sitting here staring at the wall, wondering exactly how to approach this lesson.
The reality is that this venture, describing the love of God, is impossible. There is no human way
to communicate such a thing, apart from looking at the life and work of Jesus. Jesus communicated love by being born as a human into suffering, living life as an outcast, dying for sin, and then
conquering death and offering us His victory through His resurrection. That's how God chose to
communicate His love for us.

As far as we can comprehend, *agape* is the love of God that we access through Christ by the
power of the Holy Spirit living in us. It is perfect love, to which we can respond only because Christ
first loved us.

Let's refer to the Word of God, specifically to a Scripture that is well-known throughout our
world, to both believers and nonbelievers alike:

Love (agape) is patient, love (agape) is kind.
It does not envy, it does not boast, it is not proud.

· · · · · · · · ·

It does not dishonor others, it is not self-seeking,

It is not easily angered, it keeps no record of wrongs.

Love (agape) does not delight in evil
but rejoices with the truth.

It always protects, always hopes, always perseveres.

Love (agape) never fails.

- 1 Corinthians 13:4-8a

*Agape* love is God's perfect love. God's love that disciplines and corrects, covers everything with grace, and pursues us - even through death and resurrection.

Through His perfect *agape* love, this all-knowing, wise King of ours has blessed us in unique relationships with each person of the Trinity.

**In the Spirit of love**, He has given us a **Father** who created and adopted us.

**In the Spirit of love**, He has given us a **brother** in our Lord Jesus, a true friend who died for us.

**In the Spirit of love**, He has given us a deep love and intimacy with the **Holy Spirit**, who becomes one with us.

Our lives are full of relationships that reflect God's love, and yet these relationships with humans will in no way satisfy our thirst for agape love. In an ultimate sense, we can't be satisfied with anything but God. The beautiful reality is that, through Christ, we actually can experience this thing called love here in our earthly realm.

The Greek language has many different words to describe this undefinable thing we call "love", and the Christian culture has taken hold of four words in an attempt to explore and explain this complex subject. These four words beautifully outline the relationship we have with God - in the Trinity.

The first word for love is "agape", the most prominent in Scripture and one we've already attempted to define above as the best description of God's divine love. The second word, "phileo", refers to a brotherly love; the third word, "eros", refers to a romantic love; and the fourth word, "storge", refers to the love within a family unit.

In this section of *Crown & Sword*, we will look at these terms - phileo, eros, and storge - at length to gain a better understanding of this Spirit of love we've been given. Not only will we dive into the definitions of these types of love, but we will also apply them to our personal relationships with Jesus Christ, the Holy Spirit, and God the Father. In this way, we will understand how to create a deeper intimacy with the Trinity.

There are numerous theologies regarding each of these Greek words, but rather than taking a deep theological dive, I will instead be be sharing my conclusions about each of these words based on my personal studies and experiences.

As we know and have seen in our world, love can be easily abused and perverted, so it's extremely important that as we examine these words we place the word *agape* before *philo, eros,* and *storge*. As we apply ourselves to each of these love relationships - or evaluate them within the Trinity - we must, first and foremost, acknowledge the spirit of *agape*. This is the love we've been given by God, which makes us powerful enough to love like Christ as we interact with those around us.

## DIGGING DEEPER 1

**Hebrews 2:10-12**

1. Everything exists for and because of whom?

2. How did God bring his many sons and daughters to glory?

3. Take a moment to ponder on the truth that you are one of Jesus' sisters.

4. Write a prayer reflecting on verse 11: "Both the one who makes people holy and those who are made holy are of the same family. So Jesus is not ashamed to call them brothers and sisters."

5. Write down a description of the perfect relationship between a sister and brother.

## DIGGING DEEPER 2

**Zephaniah 3:17**

1. The NIV translation says, "The LORD your God is with you, the Mighty Warrior who saves you." Record any images that these words provoke in your mind, whether in writing, drawing, song, or painting. Express and/or expand on this Scripture in any way you'd like.

2. Define some ways that you take "great delight" in a person.

3. Imagine the Lord delighting in you in a similar fashion, and write down your response.

4. Have you rebuked someone because you love them? A spouse, a friend, a child? How can a rebuke actually be evidence of love? Do you have any fears about doing this?

5. What is your favorite (joy-filled) love song? Write down some of the love songs that make you think of a certain person and write the person's name next to it. Contemplate the feelings that both the song and the person invoke in you.

6. Write out a prayer responding to the idea that God rejoices over you with singing.

## DIGGING DEEPER 3

**Romans 12:9-21**

1. "Love must be sincere." The commentary in my NIV Bible defines sincere as "true love, not pretense." Google defines pretense as:

   1. an attempt to make something that is not the case appear true. 2. a claim, especially a false or ambitious one.

   Have you ever been loved by someone with a love that is/was insincere? Pinpoint that in your mind and acknowledge it. Now, write about a time that <u>you</u> have expressed a love that was insincere to someone. What have you learned from the experience of loving someone in that way?

2. Several translations all use the same word "fervor" in verse 11. Define the word **fervor**. Do you believe you have "spiritual fervor"? If you are an introvert, or someone who is more passive in nature, or someone who is physically tired, then you might feel a sense of frustration as you try to associate with the word "fervor". What is "spiritual fervor," and where do we get it?

3. Spend some time meditating on verse 12. What I mean by "meditating" is spending some time in deep thought about the verse. Possibly even do some additional research on it, and write down your findings and response.

4. Verse 15 is crucial in our communities. To "do life together" and to know that we are not alone can make an indescribable difference. Pinpoint and write about a time when someone celebrated with you when something great happened in your life. Do the same about a time you had someone cry with you when life was hard. While you are considering these things, notice the feelings that are provoked. Take note of these as you write out your response.

5. Pray that God would grow in you the heart to apply verse 15 to your life.

6. Do you find it difficult to wish good things for people who harm you? How in the world is it possible to live out verses 17-20?

7. Google "images of coal on head." Click on any image that shows a person carrying coal on their head in a basket. Coal represents fuel for warmth, and it is a blessing in many cultures to receive coal. Verse 17 is often wrongly misinterpreted in our society. Providing food, drink, and coal for an enemy is actually a sacrifice of ourselves and a gift to our enemy. Record any thoughts you have on this concept and on any of the images you discover regarding it. (As you obey this Scripture, don't forget the balance - remember your own battlefield.)

8. This entire section of Scripture is the one I've found to be the richest in defining *storge* love, the love applied within the family - father, mother, brother, sister, and child. As you've studied this section of Scripture, write any reflections you have about living this out within your own family unit. Then write another response as you contemplate what this might look like within a church community. What action steps can you take now to apply these Scriptures to both those aspects of your life?

9. Write a prayer for the Lord's grace and strength to fall on you as you apply yourself to the work.

# CHAPTER 2

# PHILEO LOVE

. . . . . . . . . .

"A friend loveth at all times, and a brother is born for adversity."
Proverbs 17:17

FRIENDSHIP IS A BEAUTIFUL THING. WHAT WOULD WE DO without our friends?! Comrades. The people in our world who see us for who we truly are and love us anyway. Those who go out of their way to spend time with us. People who share tears and laughter and affection. A kindred spirit who does the hard stuff and the good stuff alongside you, not because they have to, but because they want to.

"Phileo" love is brotherly love. This is a love between friends, which brings people to the point of familial closeness, a love that binds hearts and lives in unique ways. While *phileo* can absolutely be present between siblings, it's often found even more strongly in friendships.

This type of love is found in friends who are looking in the same direction and have like minds and goals. They spur each other on and find strength in one another for life's journey. Experienced jointly, *agape-phileo* love makes living fun. It gives us a pure and healthy drive to press onward in life, and motivates us to enjoy the journey. The color and depth that this love brings to our life is crucial for living well.

Scripture gives us plenty of examples of such love: Barnabas and Paul, Elizabeth and Mary, Ruth and Naomi, Moses and Aaron, Elisha and Elijah, Jonathan and David, and the list goes on. Honestly, I can't name a favorite. There are too many to choose from!

. . . . . . . . .

In my life, I've been extremely blessed to have experienced a great depth of this *phileo* love. Each friendship is unique, drawing out and motivating a different part of me.

Investing in and being invested in by different women with different gifts and personalities, in different seasons of life, is one of the main reasons you and I were created. Living out this *phileo* love is a primary call on each our lives. This is what brings God glory. This love reflects our God in His passion, in His sacrifice, in His generosity, in His help, in His encouragement, and in His comradeship.

This spirit of love with which God has gifted us allows us to both receive and to give this *agape-phileo* love. Let us not live lives that are apathetic and limp, with colorless relationships. May we be a sisterhood that is active, lively, and vivid!

## DIGGING DEEPER 4

### Ruth 1

1. Examine the love Naomi expressed to her daughters-in-law when she told them to go back to their mother's home. How was it sacrificial love for her to send them away from her?

2. Re-read verse 16. Have you ever felt this passionately about someone? Write down any names that come to mind.

3. In this instance, we have a friendship that was a mentor/mentee relationship - not just related by law, but by spirit. Naomi was a spiritual mother to Ruth. We see that Ruth refers to "the LORD" (vs. 17) , not "your Lord" or "the Lord of Israel." We can assume that Naomi had taught and shown Ruth the love of God. Have you had a spiritual mother or father who has become extremely dear to you? Write a few sentences describing that relationship.

4. Verse 14 says Ruth **clung** to Naomi. Are there specific friendships that you would cling to if they were threatened? Write down the name of this person(s).

## DIGGING DEEPER 5

### 2 Timothy 1:16-18

1. "... because he often refreshed me." Do you have someone in your life who refreshes you?

2. Who are the people for whom you will go out of your way to refresh them? How do you do that?

3. Have there been times when you've felt deserted by everyone? But perhaps you had a few people who you knew had your back and were with you through it all? Write some words describing the time you felt like Paul did - deserted- but had someone like Onesiphorus.

4. Do you have friends who you feel go above and beyond to help you? Allow the gratitude to resonate in you, and make a point to communicate your appreciation to them today.

## DIGGING DEEPER 6

**Proverbs 18:24**

1. You likely have a few friendships that have proven to lack an *agape-phileo* love, and they have been unreliable. In order to grow in the spirit of power, you will need to create boundaries in your kingdom, or make sure the boundaries you have in place are steady. What does this verse say will happen soon if one relies on these unreliable friends?

2. *Phileo* has a way of making the bond with a friend so close that they become family. Many times, we lean on our friends more than our siblings. Have you experienced any friendships that have stuck just as close to you, if not closer, than a sibling?

3. Are you a person who loves with an *agape-phileo* love that is sacrificial and devoted? Prayerfully write your response.

## DIGGING DEEPER 7

**2 Kings 2:1-18**

1. Experiencing the heartbreaking news that a friend or loved one has passed away and will no longer be living in the flesh is gut-wrenching. Have you ever heard news about a friend that you knew was the truth, but didn't want to be reminded of? (verses 3 & 5) Write a few words down regarding one or two of those experiences.

2. Was Elisha's request in verse 9 a pure one, or was it a selfish one? Why would Elisha request such a thing from Elijah?

3. In what ways do you see an *agape*-covered *phileo* love displayed in this chapter?

# CHAPTER 3:

# BROTHERLY LOVE

· · · · · · · · ·

"Because I have a brother, I will always have a friend."
Unknown

JESUS CHRIST DIED SO THAT HE COULD CALL ME HIS SISTER.

I confess that even though I've known this truth for many years, the gravity of it didn't really hit me until I made it through a long season of hardship, when it was abundantly clear just how much grace I need, how weak and incompetent I really am. In my deepest darkness, Jesus came and gave me grace. He met me down in my pit, and He gave me the courage to walk out of it with Him.

There is such beauty in walking this path of life with this perfectly righteous big brother, who meets me where I am, sits with me there, gives me freedom to process, and then brings me to our Father.

My brother, Jesus, will share things with me just because He likes me and trusts me. He will laugh with me and be goofy with me, He celebrates with me and cries with me. He keeps me accountable and shares hard truths with me. And for some reason, it's easier for me to swallow a reprimand from a faithful brother than from my husband or father.

There have been many times when I have fought and overcome the fearful insecurities in my life because of this particular relationship. When accusing thoughts come at me, I can tune into the voice of my kindred spirit Jesus. My brother's and co-heir's voice might say, "Well, yes—you should

· · · · · · · ·

apologize. It's okay if she doesn't forgive you right away. I have. And don't be afraid. I'll go with you." Or maybe He will say, "You did the best you knew how to do; now that you know better—do better."

Scripture tells us we are a co-heir with Christ. Dictionary.com defines "co-heir" as: `a person who inherits jointly with others.`

Thefreedictionary.com defines "heir" as: `1. A person who inherits the estate of another. 2. A person who succeeds or is in line to succeed to a hereditary rank, title or office. 3. One who receives or is expected to receive a heritage, as of ideas, from a predecessor.`

We know that Jesus is the son of God and that He will rule over all, for eternity. We also know that Jesus is King. Now, if Jesus is Prince of Peace and promised King of eternity, and we are his brothers and sisters as the Scriptures say, if we are actually **coheirs**, then we will inherit the eternal kingdom and throne **jointly** with Jesus.

Deep breath.

Mind blown and heart busted.

Do you believe it? Have you embraced this truth? Do you sense the weight and freedom of the power that this title has given you when you accepted Jesus as your Savior?

The drama on the ground wants to rock any confidence we have about being co-heirs with Christ. Even if you **are** a co-heir with Christ, if you don't believe and walk in that identity, then the power you hold becomes limp and you're rendered much less effective. Embracing our identity in Christ is key to keeping our feet planted and our stature in an upright position. I can **know** that I'm co-heir with Christ all day, but if I'm not also **believing** and **walking** in that truth, then my victory is so limited.

Can you believe that our brother, the Lord Jesus, asks us to participate in the building of His kingdom!? Oh yes, He will sit on high on the judgment seat. But my relationship with Him is sound. I can have humble confidence in His love and respect for me as I approach that throne. We've laughed together. We've cried and sang and danced together. Jesus Christ has sacrificed His all and washed me clean from my sin—all in order to be my best friend and brother, and to gift me with the title **co-heir**.

## DIGGING DEEPER 8

### John 2:1-11

1.  Picture Jesus at a wedding feast. Is He serious and disapproving of all the celebration and laughter around him? Or is He drinking and laughing and conversing? Is He the one telling

jokes, or is He listening and laughing beside his disciples? Does He start conversations with those He doesn't know? Is it awkward or easy conversation, or intriguing and entertaining? Write a few sentences about your thoughts.

2. Why would Mary tell Jesus, "They have no more wine"? Imagine the things she's seen Jesus do as she raised Him up in her home. He was fully human, and the time for Him to do miracles was precise and anything but thoughtless. Yet, Mary undoubtedly knew and saw the power her son had as the Son of God. I sense her tone and words being spoken behind her eyes: "You need to do something about this." I also see the smile that tickled her lips at the anticipation of Jesus' solution. Can you imagine yourself as Mary in verses 4 and 5? Would you have behaved differently or in a similar way?

3. Does putting yourself at the wedding with Jesus in this setting change your perspective of Him at all? How?

4. Do you think you would've enjoyed sitting at His table? Explain.

5. Has Jesus ever turned something rather ordinary in your life into something extraordinary? Write down an event in your life where Jesus did something delightful for you.

# DIGGING DEEPER 9

## Matthew 14:1-23

1. John the Baptist was a blood relative to Jesus. Their mothers were close, and there is a chance that the two had spent time together as boys. John had baptized Jesus and proclaimed Jesus' name, pointing many toward the Son of God. What was Jesus' response when He heard about the atrocity of John's execution?

2. How did Jesus respond to the crowd when He saw them, even in the depth of His sorrow?

3. How do verses 22-23 show Jesus protecting His tired disciples and establishing a boundary line in love?

4. Reflect on how the Son of God made time to mourn and spend time with the Father. How does this reflect the humanity of Christ?

## DIGGING DEEPER 10

### John 4:3-30

1. A Samaritan woman would be someone with whom the average Jew would never converse. We know that Jesus was no ordinary Jew - no ordinary person, in fact. The tired man spoke with this woman anyway, and actually made a request. Do you ever feel surprised that God would talk to and want anything from you? Explain.

2. In my mind, the dialogue between Jesus and the Samaritan woman in these verses is similar to a banter, seasoned with amusement, perhaps even sarcasm, awe, conviction, and delight. Jesus exposes the woman's misdeeds, yet there seems to be no hint of shame or condemnation here. Have you ever felt the conviction of an exposed sin drawn out by the *phileo* love of Jesus? Although you felt the depth of the wrong, shame was not in the picture, and you felt no need to get defensive. If so, write about it. If not, write any observations you have made about the dialogue here.

3. Write about a time when you have been so delighted by what Jesus had revealed to you that you eagerly went out to tell others.

## DIGGING DEEPER 11

### John 15:12-17

1. Would you say that you are a friend of Jesus? Why?

2. What is the difference between a friend and a servant? Why is it important for you to know and believe that you are not just a servant of Jesus, but actually His friend?

3. Why did God choose you to be His friend?

4. What does verse 16 say that the Father will give to you? Why?

5. What do verses 12 and 17 have in common? What would it look like, practically, for you personally to obey Jesus' command in the day to day of your life?

# DIGGING DEEPER 12

## Romans 8:17

1. Does defining the words "heir" and "co-heir" have any impact on the way you receive this verse? Does it change the way you view yourself in any way? If so, how?

2. In order to share in Christ's glory as a co-heir, what must we do?

3. Sharing in Christ's sufferings does not mean we need to inflict pain on ourselves. Suffering is part of the natural course of every human life. To share in Christ's suffering, we simply live a human life. The difference in the Christian's life is that we proclaim Jesus **while** we suffer, and we receive eternal hope and glory as a result. How does it encourage you to know that your suffering isn't just to bring God glory, but also to receive glory with Him? Write a prayer reflecting on this verse.

# CHAPTER 4:

# EROS LOVE

• • • • • • • • • •

"We rejoice and delight in you; we will praise your love more than wine."
Song of Solomon 1:4

*EROS* LOVE IS THE LEAST TALKED ABOUT IN CHRISTIAN CULture. Yet it's one we shouldn't skim over. The Greek word "eros" is mostly used in reference to romantic and sexual affections. This word is used once in the Greek translation of the Hebrew Bible in Proverbs 7:18, and it isn't in the Koine (most used) Greek text of the New Testament.

Although we might not find the actual word "eros" in the much of Biblical text, there is no question that the idea is addressed. The whole book of Song of Solomon touches on this concept. Many say that Song of Solomon (also called Song of Songs) contains symbolism for something deeper, and I agree. However, to deny the sensual tone of the text is really just silly. Scriptures contain many instructions for handling eros love, throughout both the Old and New Testaments.

Sexuality is a powerful and mysterious force. The mishandling of it can do such damage that most people don't like to approach the subject openly. I'd like to consider eros love openly, but first I want to clarify that this subject does include, but is not limited to, sex. The word "eros" does connect to the words "erotic" and "ecstasy", but so many definitions of this love begin and end with those or similar words. In reality, sex is merely an aspect of eros love, not the fullness of it.

I thoroughly enjoyed C.S. Lewis' explanation of this love in his book *The Four Loves*. True eros love isn't lust or the passion of sexual relations, which is what many automatically think of.

• • • • • • •

Eros is the desire *for someone*, not just what they can give. Eros love is enraptured with the person as a whole, and is just as satisfied with giving as receiving. It isn't just the appearance of a person that ignites and fuels Eros love, but *all* the attributes of the person who is loved.

Eros is the most mysterious and inexplicable of the loves. It is also the most mishandled and dangerous love, apart from *agape*. But join this eros love, filled with passion and longing and enjoyment, with the *agape* love of God, and we have a divine gift.

## DIGGING DEEPER 13

### Genesis 4:1 & Nahum 1:7

1. Read these verses in the King James Version.

2. In the original Hebrew text the word "yada" is used in both these verses: "Adam 'yada' (knew) Eve," and "The Lord 'yada' (knows) those who trust in Him." The biblical love we are discussing relates much more closely to intimacy than a physical sexual act. Is it possible that the way Adam knew Eve is a cloudy reflection of how God knows us? Expand on those thoughts in writing.

3. I'd encourage you to research the word more and write out some notes. Blueletterbible.com is a fantastic free resource to do word studies like this.

## DIGGING DEEPER 14

### Genesis 29:18-20

1. Describe a time that you did something fairly unpleasant, but it wasn't a challenge for you because of the love you held for the person on the other side of the work.

2. Have you ever felt a sort of infatuation or had a crush, which made going about your daily toil more enjoyable? Delightful thoughts about a certain person rolling around your head and thrilling feelings in your heart can somehow give an upbeat soundtrack to the day to day. If you can recall feeling this way, define a few of those moments in your journal.

3. Imagine that those feelings could be similar to the way the Holy Spirit delights in you. Write a prayerful response.

# DIGGING DEEPER 15

**Proverbs 5:18 & 19**

1.  Have you ever thought that being "intoxicated" (NIV), "ravished" (KJV), "enraptured" (NKJ), or "captivated" (NLT) by a person was unbiblical? If so, what gave you that impression?

2.  Google defines "ravish" as: `fill (someone) with intense delight; enrapture.` Compose a prayer thanking God for the blessing of such feelings and experiences. Pray that God would bring you a better understanding of what *agape-eros* love is. Pray that He would heal you from any experiences of this eros love being mishandled in your life. Ask God to bless your future experiences of being intoxicated with a man's love.

3.  Please join me in prayer for our church. Let us pray that we, the church, would be able to find the balance between dishonoring the sacred beauty of eros love and treating it as unapproachable at the other extreme.

# DIGGING DEEPER 16

**Proverbs 30:18**

1.  We have science that explains the four concepts being presented here. But understanding how the science was designed and the force that makes it so is something completely outside our comprehension. Write down a few adjectives to describe the "way of a man with a young woman."

2.  The differences between male and female humans are astounding. When a man and a woman unify in communication or teamwork, it really is something to behold. Compose a prayer asking that God would prompt wonder and amazement in you as you experience or witness "the way of a man with a woman." I don't mean only within the intimate encounter of sex, but also in any positive exchange between man and woman. (Even if you are a single woman, this is still a very worthwhile prayer!)

CHAPTER 5:

# PRINCESS BRIDE

· · · · · · · · ·

"To fall in love with God is the greatest romance; to seek Him the greatest adventure; to find Him, the greatest human achievement."

St. Augustine of Hippo

IT HAS BEEN SAID THAT GOD IS THE LOVER OF OUR SOULS. This was fairly easy for me to grasp and wholeheartedly believe as a young single woman. I would make candlelit dinners on Valentine's Day to celebrate with Jesus. Some might say I was cheesy, while others might call me passionate; I'll own both.

However, once I had a tangible lover, it became difficult to keep the Holy Spirit as the true love of my heart. After about 7 years of marriage, that jealous Holy Spirit got a bit more aggressive and really pursued me. He revealed some lies I'd been believing and wooed me back to Him.

Our husbands and physical lovers are a phenomenal gift from God, and yet it is common to hold them at a place in our hearts that is meant only for the Holy Spirit. We end up placing expectations on our men to fill certain needs of our souls, needs which they are not capable of fulfilling. Only our God can fill all our soul's needs.

Our God has come to give us eros in its purest and richest forms. ***We become a treasured princess bride when we embrace the honor He's offering us with this perfect love.***

Having the Spirit as the lover of our soul is thrilling. It's a consuming feeling of adoration and deepth. The love that the Holy Spirit brings, *agape-eros*, reaches the deepest part of our hearts and imparts new life to us. He sees us in our raw nakedness, and He sees beauty. The Holy Spirit takes

· · · · · · · ·

our hearts and minds to great and beautiful places with such gentleness, honoring us perfectly as His bride.

As we learn to look to Him to fulfill our spiritual needs, we will never be disappointed. When we know Him this way, we can't help but respond by being thrilled, comforted, exhilarated, safe, rested, and grateful.

He is always tender, always providing us with refuge, always pursuing our hearts. He is a jealous lover, but He also gives us freedom beyond measure. He waits for us. He fights for us. And when we respond to what the Holy Spirit desires to give us, we will never be in want. Our hearts can be completely satisfied. Our intimate relations with Him leads to fruit spilling forth in our lives. And we become a princess-bride who is radiant and abundant with life.

## DIGGING DEEPER 17

### Isaiah 54:5 & 62:5

1. Surely you've heard the phrase "the church is the bride of Christ." Have you ever made this concept more personal, placing the Lord Almighty as **your** spiritual husband? Write down your response.

2. Some definitions that Merriam-Webster.com gives for the word "redeemer" include: *a person who brings goodness, honor, etc., to something again: a person who redeems something. [Or perhaps "someone?"] Synonyms: deliverer, savior, rescuer, defender, guard, guardian, keeper, lookout, protector, etc.* Write down any other adjectives you can think of to describe your God, your Spiritual Redeemer. (If you are in an intimate relationship with a man that does not include any of these traits, not echoing any of God's character, seek Christian counsel immediately.)

## DIGGING DEEPER 18

### Song of Songs 2:4-7

1. Have you ever delighted and feasted so much in love that you became overwhelmed to the point of exhaustion?

2. Have you ever been in prayer or worship or fellowship with the Lord and felt overwhelmed by His presence?

3. In Watchman Nee's book *The Song of Songs: The Divine Romance Between God and Man,* he says these things regarding verse 7:

The daughters of Jerusalem love excitement, and they love to meddle with many things. Therefore, the Lord tells them not to stir up the maiden.

The King gives this charge because the maiden has become sick of love. There is no need to stir her up any more; she can pause a little while. She is in the Lord's hand, and there is no need for others to arouse her. If others try to meddle with her affairs, it will not help her. Instead it will only stir her up. Wait for her to rise by herself. Do not think that she is too soulish and that she needs help. This is where her lessons have brought her, and there should be a pause. Love has reached its climax. The King is present; therefore, be still (Hab 2:20). (pg 28/29)

Write down any thoughts you have in response to Watchman Nee's statements.

4. Can you recall ever being in a place where you needed to rest in the presence of the King, but others were trying to stir you up to do more? **IF** you can relate, write a few words about that experience.

5. Can you recall a time that you behaved like a "Daughter of Jerusalem," trying to stir up or awaken love before it desires, either in yourself or another? Write a few words in response.

## DIGGING DEEPER 19
························································

### Song of Songs 8:5-7

1. I must also share with you what Watchman Nee says about these verses! He interprets verse 6 like this:

"The heart is the place of love, while the arm is the place of strength. 'Set me as permanently as a seal upon Your heart, and as indelibly as a seal upon Your arm. Just as the priests bore the Israelites upon their breasts and their shoulders, remember me constantly in Your heart and sustain me with Your arm. I know that I am weak and empty, and I am conscious of my powerlessness. Lord, I am a helpless person. If I try to preserve myself until Your coming, it will only bring shame to Your name and loss to myself. All my hopes are in Your love and power.'" (pg 119)

How does Watchman Nee's interpretation give you a better sense of the passion behind the words written in verse 6?

········

2. Watchman Nee also writes the following:

"Verse 7 says, 'Many waters cannot quench love, neither can the floods drown it: if a man would give all the substance of his house for love, it would utterly be contemned.' 'Many waters' signify trials that believers go through. 'Floods' signify persecutions from the enemy. His love and the fire of His love cannot be drowned by persecutions. If He loves us, no trial or persecution can do anything to us. This love cannot be bought with money. In other words it is irreplaceable....we will not earn His love with more work, busy times, or toiling services. We can only offer ourselves to Him so that we will become the object of His love." (pg 121)

Have you ever felt love that seemed to consume you like a fire consumes things? Perhaps you have a relationship where you have experienced a large amount of tension and trials, and yet you both still chose to be faithful to one another--there was still a flame that just wouldn't go out. If you have any relationships like that, write those people down.

3. Have you ever thought of the Holy Spirit as a lover, pursuing you? As a good and faithful Spirit who gives you good things, just to delight you? Who stays by your side, holding you up when the going gets tough? Who chooses to faithfully wait for you if you choose something or someone else over Him for a time? Prayerfully write a response to these thoughts.

4. Write out Song of Songs 8:6 & 7.

5. Pray that you'd be open to receive the Holy Spirit's love in an intimate way that would move you into a deeper passion for Him.

# CHAPTER 6:

# STORGE LOVE

∴ ∴ ∴ ∴ ∴

"See what great love the Father has lavished on us,
that we should be called children of God."
1 John 3:1

THE GREAT I AM. YAHWEH. THE CREATOR OF EVERYTHING. The King of Kings and Lord of Lords. The Holiest of Holies.

In Jewish culture many people will not even utter the name of Yahweh. Their reverence for this infinite and magnificent Almighty Lord is great - as it should be.

Yet as a Christ-follower, we also know that Yahweh put aside His majesty and embraced humanity as Jesus Christ. He stepped into a limited and frail body similar to ours and bore our filth so that we might be worthy to come before Him. And not only come before Him, but climb into His lap and be enfolded into His arms.

This is pure *agape*. Because of this *agape* love, we have been adopted as God's daughters. He has taken us in as His very own, and in this way He reveals to us *agape-storge* love.

C.S. Lewis described storge love as something like the feelings of being covered with a blanket, or the comfortable joy of sitting on the porch and seeing a toy out on the lawn.

Storge love is the love that resides in the family. It's the natural affection or bond between mother, father, and siblings.

In its purest form, storge love embodies both comfort and honor. In true storge love, there should be a respect for the ones cherished, and a high value placed on the relationships that dwell in this safe place.

Because of sinful humans perverting and abusing this kind of love in our world, our understanding of this is most likely skewed. The only complete truth regarding this love is offered to us in the Word of God.

It's astounding to me how our Lord offers *agape-storge* as a healing salve. He readily and perfectly fills the missing gaps of our humanity when we choose to embrace Him.

*"Because you are His sons, God sent the Spirit of His Son into our hearts, the Spirit who calls out 'Abba Father."* Galatians 4:6

## DIGGING DEEPER 20

### John 1:12-13

1. "He gave the right to become children of God." The Greek word that was translated as "right" in this passage is "exousia". It can also be translated as "power, authority, liberty, jurisdiction, and strength". One definition said that it is **power of choice, liberty of doing as one pleases.** How does one come to acquire this "right"? Have you claimed this right? Do you exercise this right, choosing to be a child of God on a regular basis? Expand on your answers.

2. According to the definition above, it seems that even if one has received Christ as their Savior, God still gives them a choice to become a child of His. Is possible to believe and still choose to not live as a child of God? Explain your response to that thought.

3. "Children" in this verse is translated from the Greek word "teknon", meaning: `the name trans-ferred to that intimate and reciprocal relationship formed between men by the bonds of love, friendship, trust, just as between parents and children.` My mind is drawn to the word "reciprocal" in this definition. God has given us the right and the power to have an intimate relationship with Him, a relationship defined by words like love, friendship, and trust. He has given those things to us, as we choose to be a child of His, and those things need to be reciprocated. Do you feel as though your relationship with God includes you reciprocating these things back to Him? Explain.

4. Verse 13 says that these children of His were not born due to anyone else's decision. He chose you. Therefore, no one else has authority over His relationship with you, as His child. Write out a response.

5. How would the church look any different if everyone really believed this about themselves and the other believers they bumped into? What kinds of things would change?

## DIGGING DEEPER 21

**Romans 8:15 & 16**

1. Write down what you understand slavery and bondage to be.

2. Describe what it means to be a daughter.

3. Write about any experience or understanding you have about adoption.

4. The word "Abba" is defined in the Vine's Expository Dictionary the following way: **Abba** is an Aramaic word, found in Mark 14:36, Romans 8:15, and Galatians 4:6. In the Gemara (a Rabbinical commentary on the Mishna, the traditional teaching of the Jews) it is stated that slaves were forbidden to address the head of the family by this title.. "Abba" is the word framed by the lips of infants, and betokens unreasoning trust; "father" expresses an intelligent apprehension of the relationship. The two together express the love and intelligent confidence of the child. According to this definition, are you comfortable calling God "Abba Father"?

5. Verse 15 says that the Spirit testifies that we are God's children. Does it comfort you in any way to know that you are not alone when you claim to be a child of God? That you have His Holy Spirit affirming all those thoughts, feelings, and words?

6. How does believing this truth as you live your life affect the way that you interact with others?

## DIGGING DEEPER 22

**Malachi 2:10**

1. "Do we not all have one Father? Did not one God create us?" Answer these questions and expand your answers.

2. Not everyone believes in God the Father the way you do. There are people who have chosen not to believe God. Yet, God still created them. How should we treat something/someone that God created?

3. Although the intimate *agape-storge* love cannot be shared with unbelievers, we must always respect and honor those that God has made. Describe any differences you have come across in your relationships with those inside the fellowship of believers versus those outside this fellowship.

4. What are some things that might cause the family of believers to be unfaithful to one another?

5. Love is not without conflict. How do you think you might be able to walk in the faithful comfort of *agape-storge* love through the conflict that inevitably happens within family relationships, even with brothers and sisters in Christ?

## DIGGING DEEPER 23

### Galatians 3:26-29

1. Write down these verses.

2. How can remembering this passage prompt storge love for your God and other believers around you? Explain.

3. How does one clothe oneself with Christ? Are you clothed in Christ right now?

# CHAPTER 7:

# ENCOUNTERING THE KING

· · · · · · · ·

SITTING INDIAN-STYLE ON THE GROUND IN THE DISTANCE IS A LITTLE girl. Slowly her hands move in the mud and dirt around her. She is occupied, yet there seems to be no clear motive to her activity.

She is seemingly comfortable with the mud smeared on her face and clothes. Her bare feet, matted hair, and dirt-caked fingernails are what she knows—and part of who she is.

Far off, a figure, large and radiant starts moving. As he gets closer, his regal details become more defined. His incredible size and brightness are intimidating, and yet he also embodies a sense of comfort, a warmth and kindness.

Being the essence of clean goodness, this figure walks up to the little girl and crouches down. He moves so close that his nose is almost brushing against hers. Their eyes connect, and he smiles.

In this moment, she has a choice. Looking back down at her mud pie, she avoids eye contact, even though his face is right in front of hers. Ignoring him, she continues to play with her mud pie. The kingly spirit starts to back away—he knows her heart and thoughts. He will give her room and wait in the distance until she's ready to look his way.

· · · · · · · ·

*But when he starts to retreat, she realizes that she desperately wants him near. Turning her face up she searches, the feeling of panic rushes through her at the thought of him leaving. Her eyes are greeted with a grin.*

*Smiling back she instantly drops her mud. His great joy is undeniable! It's a joy that only comes from a father as he looks upon his daughter. A delightful warmth overcomes her at the realization that he adores her.*

*Gleefully throwing her hand around his great neck he twirls her around. Her giggles harmonize beautifully with his chesty chuckle.*

*As this scene unfolds, the dirt that has been smeared over her face and crusted on her feet disappears with his touch. The light of the kingly figure envelops her as she is in his arms. Her skin becomes radiant, her rags turn to loveliness, her eyes are filled with joy and hope, while the knots matted up against her head become beautiful, cascading locks of hair.*

*She has become a new creation. The Great King has taken her up as his own and is ready to crown her with a title. Princess. He takes such delight in her. And she rejoices in Him—her great Abba Father.*

"As long as an heir is underage, he is no different than a slave, although he owns the whole estate. The heir is subject to guardians and trustees until the time set by His father. So also, when we were underage, we were in slavery under the elemental spiritual forces of the world. But when the set time had fully come, God sent His Son, born of a woman, born under the law, to redeem those under the law, that we might receive adoption to sonship. Because you are His sons, God sent the Spirit of His Son into our hearts, the Spirit who calls out, "Abba, Father." So you are no longer a slave, but God's child; and since you are His child, God has made you also an heir."

Galatians 4:1-7

## DIGGING DEEPER 24

### Galatians 4:1-7

1.  What do you think "in bondage under the elements of the world" means? The word "world" here is "kosmos" in the Greek. Knowing this helped me grasp this verse a bit more - perhaps it will help you, too.

2.  What is the difference between those that are "under the law" and those that have "sonship"?

3.  How does the description of the girl "encountering the King" reflect this verse?

## DIGGING DEEPER 25

### 2 Corinthians 1:3-7

1.  Mirriam-Webster's Dictionary defines "compassion" in the following way: `sympathetic consciousness of others' distress together with a desire to alleviate it.` Why would Paul call God the "Father of compassion"?

2.  Why would Paul call God "the God of all comfort"?

3.  How does verse 4 relate to this storge love we are studying?

4.  Consider what sufferings of Christ you share with Him.

5.  Identify some times when you have experienced the comfort that abounds through Christ.

6.  I believe what Paul speaks about in verses 6 and 7 reveals how the power of Christ works in us to love how Christ loves. Would you agree? How do these verses reflect the agape love of God?

## DIGGING DEEPER 26

### Philippians 4:19-20

1.  Our earthly fathers may or may not try to provide for all our needs. They never will be able to do so perfectly. But our God can and will. His riches are glorious and perfect. And He is wise, always knowing what is best for us. Write out a prayer centered around these verses.

Now, may our Lord Jesus Christ Himself,

And our God and Father,

Who has loved us and given us

Everlasting consolation and good hope by grace,

Comfort your hearts and establish you

in every good word and work.

~ 2 Thessalonians 2:16-17

# PART IV:

# THE DISCIPLINED WARRIOR

· · · · · · · · ·

We have been given a spirit of discipline.

## THE MISSION:

*Engage in the spiritual war with a disciplined, sound mind.*

· · · · · · · · ·

# CHAPTER 1

# WARRIORS ARE DISCIPLINED

· · · · · · · · · ·

" It was character that got us out of bed, commitment that moved us into action, and discipline that enabled us to follow through."

Zig Zaglar

2 TIMOTHY 1:7 SAYS THAT WE HAVE BEEN GIVEN A SPIRIT OF "sophronismos". This Greek word "sophronismos" communicates an "admonishing or calling to soundness of mind, to moderation and self-control." (Blueletterbible.com)

Ladies, we have authority and a royal position as a daughter, sister, and princess bride. Yet there is still a battle raging.

God did not give us a crown and then ask us to sit down beside Him and put our feet up. No one would never describe a God-seeking, Spirit-filled life as easy. **Rewarding**, for sure, but not **easy**. A woman who is actively pursuing God will rarely find herself bored or unchallenged. She is constantly growing and learning. She's not perfect by any means, but she's working towards excellence, with her eyes on her king. She is diligent and disciplined.

Romans 8:13 & 14 in The Message translation states:

· · · · · · · ·

God's Spirit beckons. There are things to do and places to go! This resurrection life you received from God is not a timid, grave-tending life. It's adventurously expectant, greeting God with a child-like, "What's next Papa?"

As a young woman I would recite 2 Timothy 1:7 with a translation that used the word "discipline" for "sophronismos". It was encouraging and kept me moving forward in my day to day.

Yet as I grew older, and the demands of my life changed, the translations of the Bible that expressed that word "sophronismos" by using "sound mind" have suited my soul much better. With raging hormones and rowdy boys and the constant demands of family, knowing that God has given me a mind that is, well, *clear* and not crazy - that is a truth I cling to!

1 Corinthians 14:33 says, "God is not a God of confusion, but of peace."

The knowledge that God is not a God of confusion and that He has given me the mind of Christ (1 Corinthians 2:16) puts me at ease when my physical mind and emotions do not feel completely right at any given time. Knowing this truth helps me to lean back, rather than acting rashly, and trust the Lord to lead me in truth. Even this act, though, of trusting the mind of Christ in me, takes discipline.

In order for one to bear the title "Warrior", one would need to be disciplined by nature. Dictionary.com gives the following characteristics of a warrior: `a person engaged or experienced in warfare; soldier or a person who shows or has shown great vigor, courage, or aggressiveness.`

Whether we want to acknowledge it or not, we are fighting a battle. The battle of good versus evil rages all around us and inside of us. Anyone who is old enough to read these words has encountered this struggle and is either currently engaged in or has at one time experienced this warfare. That qualifies you as a warrior. The question remains, though: have you shown great vigor, courage, or aggressiveness in overcoming the bad things that come against or well up within you?

When it comes to battling the world, Satan, and our flesh, we are ineffective unless we have the power of God within us. A person cannot "be good" all the time, just because it's the right thing to do. We might be able to outwardly obey, but only for a short time in our own strength. To truly be victorious, we must engage in this war with the power we've been given through Christ.

True warriors don't obey simply for the sake of following an order; instead, they apply themselves with discipline, honor, and great passion of heart.

"Warriors are driven by an internal eternal mandate.
Their response is ordered from within. This means

they will give all that is in their power to give.
There is an overflow in their response..."
From *Girls with Swords* by Lisa Bevere

## DIGGING DEEPER 1

........................................

**Romans 12:11**

1. The Greek word here for "zeal" is "spoude" meaning *earnestness in accomplishing, promoting, or striving after anything.* Would you say that you have spiritual zeal? Why would such a thing be important to God?

2. "Keeping your spiritual fervor" could refer to the fervor that the Holy Spirit provides, or it could refer to building up the determination and passion in our soul for spiritual matters. The Greek word here for "fervor" means *to boil with heat.* Write out three ways that you could practically apply yourself to the instruction in this verse.

## DIGGING DEEPER 2

........................................

**2 Corinthians 3:12**

1. Write out this verse.

2. Read Exodus 34:29-35 and then 2 Corinthians 3:7-11. Write a short summary of the verses in 2 Corinthians.

3. What is the hope we have that should make us bold?

## DIGGING DEEPER 3

........................................

**Proverbs 28:1**

1. The Greek word for "bold" here refers to *confidence, trust, free of care, security, and hope.* (blueletterbible.com) If we have entered the New Covenant with Christ, we are considered righteous, and therefore, according to this verse, we are bold. Examine your behavior and demeanor in the season you are in right now. Determine whether or not you've been acting as a righteous woman with boldness, and then write a prayerful response.

........

2. Wikipedia says that wild male lions have a lifespan of only 10-14 years, as opposed to the 20 years they might live in captivity. The shorter life span in the wild is a result of continual fighting with rival males. It appears that lions are unafraid of a fight. List some similarities between lions and the Christian warrior.

# CHAPTER 2

# THE MEEK WARRIOR

· · · · · · · · ·

"I still remain convinced that truth, love peaceableness, meekness, & kindness are the violence which can master all other violence. The world will be theirs as soon as ever sufficient number of people with purity of heart, with strength, & with perseverance, think & live out the thoughts of love & truth, of meekness & peaceableness."

~Albert Schweitzer

GOD, THE ORIGINAL WARRIOR (EXODUS 15:3), PUTS WORDS like "meek" and "warrior" next to one another. Humanity might not. Yet as we look to Jesus, who is ultimately God and all-powerful, we see that He chose to use his power meekly.

Jesus was disciplined enough to submit to his Father God, with whom He is one and equal. He obeyed even to the point of death, curbing His power in order to deliver us all.

As a royal co-heir with Christ, we too are called to act meekly. The power and authority we've been given comes with the responsibility to follow our brother Jesus in obedience to our heavenly Father. In this we honor our King in all things, looking to the eternal glory rather than the momentary victory.

· · · · · · · ·

Many times, having victory in our ground battles means battles lost in the air. Being "right" about something or winning an argument might feel great momentarily, but the way we respond and the way we fight impacts more than the immediate.

Our God has ordained a specific chain of command. We see it all over His creation. We see it in the angels, in nature, in government and business, and we see it in churches. In order to honor God, we must honor the chain of command.

God is the one who gives authority, and to obey God means we must honor those in authority over us, whether or not we appreciate or agree with them.

Lisa Bevere wrote about honor in her book *Girls with Swords*: "There is no way to separate a true warrior from honor, because warriors are honor-bound to something higher than themselves. The mighty samurai lived this discipline, and the medieval knights practiced chivalry. Honor meant they complied with stringent codes that required commitment and discipline."

Submission is an act of discipline, and it is the act that led to our salvation.

> "During the days of Jesus' life on earth, he offered
> up prayers and petitions with fervent cries and tears
> to the one who could save him from his death, and
> he was heard because of his reverent submission.
> Son though he was, he learned obedience from what
> he suffered and, once made perfect, he became the
> source of eternal salvation for all who obey him."
> -Hebrews 5:7-9

Anne, a wise sister of mine, said that this Scripture reminded her of the importance of learning to be obedient even when it's hard: "Jesus asked God to save Him from His fate, and God heard Him, but didn't save His son because He had a far greater purpose: ETERNAL SALVATION FOR ALL!! If we keep being obedient, God's greater purpose will be revealed through us, in us. Hang in there, girls, stay the course, and keep obeying. You will learn so much, and God will do amazing things."

## DIGGING DEEPER 4

### Luke 22:24-30

1. Pinpoint a time that you were in a dispute with someone(s), either internally or externally over who was the greatest.

2. Examine a leader in your life who you admire. List a few traits about them that you like.

3. Is this leader you admire a person who lords their position and authority over those they lead, or do they *serve* the people they have authority over?

4. Do you believe that when you serve Jesus by serving those around you, that you will be rewarded?

5. Why should the reward *not* be our only reason for serving? Have you ever been tempted to make the reward the whole reason you serve? Explain.

6. If you were to live life desiring to serve, would you get sad if you weren't recognized? Would you ever be disappointed that there was no opportunity to serve?

## DIGGING DEEPER 5

### Luke 22:42

1. What is the "cup" Jesus is asking God to take from Him?

2. If Jesus was God, wouldn't His will be the same as the Father's? Explain your answer.

3. How does Jesus, equal with the Father, provide the perfect picture of submission?

4. Recall what you know of Jesus' life and write what you remember of His behavior regarding submission. Who did He submit to in his human lifetime? Who did he NOT submit to? End your answer with a sentence summing up Jesus' pattern of submission.

5. Is there an authority in your life who is asking you to do something contrary to your convictions, or is leading in a way that you don't agree with? What is the Lord's instruction on handling yourself in this matter? Prayerfully answer that question. Refer to biblical examples such as Esther, King David with Saul, Abigail, etc.

## DIGGING DEEPER 6

### John 13:3-17

1. I really appreciate the way that the New Living Translation says "Jesus knew that the Father had given him authority over everything, and that he had come from God and would return to God; **so** he got up…" WHY was Jesus okay with washing feet? Did this action disgrace Him or make Him less God because it was the job of the lowest servant?

2. There was no servant there who washed the men's feet when they came in. And none of the disciples volunteered for the job, because it would be admitting that they were "inferior." Why did Jesus do it Himself instead of instructing someone else to do the job?

3. Jesus did the job completely. In this study about becoming a warrior, I am referring to the discipline to actually **do**. It's a call to action. Do the thing, and do it completely. Write down all the steps Scripture describes that Jesus took when washing the disciples' feet.

4. This was an extremely awkward situation in this culture, to have the teacher/master washing feet. Have you ever chosen **not** to serve someone in a situation where it would be awkward and uncomfortable?

5. Did you notice that Judas was at the table? The text plainly says that Jesus knew about Judas' betrayal. Did Jesus choose to skip Judas as He was going around the table to wash feet? Write out some of your thoughts regarding this.

6. What position does Jesus say is the greatest?

## DIGGING DEEPER 7

...........................................................

### Matthew 5:5

1. Research the word "meek." Find and write out three different definitions.

2. What are some common misconceptions concerning this word?

3. Describe one way that Jesus modeled meekness.

4. What does Jesus mean when He said that the meek will "inherit the earth"?

5. What are two ways you will display meekness in the next 24 hours?

CHAPTER 3:

# TO THE LETTER

• • • • • • • • • •

"Well-behaved women rarely make history."
Laurel Thatcher Ulrich

THERE IS A TIME TO SUBMIT, AND THERE IS A TIME TO RESIST.
Sometimes following the rules too closely can reap destruction. As a Royal Warrior, we must be sensitive to the moment by moment leading of the Holy Spirit in order to know what we should do at any given time.

I look at Acts 4:19 and I see Peter and John "talk back" to the government authorities. I study Abigail in the Old Testament, a woman who goes against her husband for the greater good. I see the cultural circumstances that form the backdrop during New Testament time and then read Paul's letters, which speak of the woman's role being more equal, and I find… God is not so very black and white.

There is a time to go with the flow and a time to go against the grain. How do we discern which is which? We listen and lean into our God. Our perfect Father, Brother, and Husband will guide the way.

Most of the time, I've found that God's call is to submission. We are called to be David in the cave: he finds his enemy, who is also his king, popping a squat right in front of him, and yet David extends honor and mercy. Most of the time, our call means following Jesus as He is willingly led from the garden by guards.

• • • • • • • •

There are times, though, when God fills us with His Spirit and we are called to be like Peter and John in Acts 4, when they boldly argued with religious leaders. The Sanhedrin saw their courage and "became astonished, taking note that they'd been with Jesus."

Paul, a prolific author of the New Testament, broke the rules of the old covenant. In 2 Corinthians 3:6 he refers to "the letter that kills", meaning the law that led to guilt. Paul moved away from the Old Testament, he submitted to God's calling through the grace of the Holy Spirit in the new covenant. After a miraculous encounter with God, Paul went against the Pharisees and the teachings he'd known and had followed all his life, becoming a great leader in Christ's church. Later, he joined the other apostles and worked with them, respectfully submitting to them.

Jesus had a woman thrown before Him who had been caught in the act of adultery. The letter of the law said that she should be stoned to death. The leaders asked Jesus what they should do, and in response Jesus said, "Let any one of you who is without sin be the first to throw the stone at her." Our God did something outside the law. Jesus created a new law and covenant. And this Jesus, who gives us this new grace-filled covenant, is our Commander.

We are called to submit to our Lord. As warriors in the unseen battle, we must respect the God-given authority that is established over us. Whether they are younger in age or faith, whether they are schooled or unschooled, we are to submit to those God has put in authority. Let's trust the Holy Spirit to prompt us if we ever need to take any action outside of where our leader would direct.

Likewise, we must honor God by serving, respecting and loving others when we are the chosen authority.

Warriors are dedicated not just to the rules, but to a higher cause, and along the journey they irresistibly call others to join them.

We must learn to balance discipline and grace. The letter kills, but the Spirit gives life. Let us be warriors who are disciplined in following the Spirit of life to the end of ourselves. May honoring our Lord be of the utmost importance as we exercise freedom within who He made us to be, applying ourselves to the course He has for us!

## DIGGING DEEPER 8

### I Samuel 24:3-22

1. If you are unfamiliar with the relationship between Saul and David in Scripture, do some research or ask someone who has some biblical knowledge to inform you about it. (1 Samuel is filled with the history of these two men. It's a fantastic book of stories, not just about these men, but also about many of our ancestors and our faith.)

2. Do you believe David did the right thing in this encounter?

3. If you were one of David's followers, what might you have thought about David's actions? Why did his men submit to David's lead?

4. Why do you think David behaved the way he did?

## DIGGING DEEPER 9

**Numbers 12**

1. Have you ever found yourself speaking against one of the Lord's servants?

2. According to this Scripture, what can we assume God thinks about such dishonor?

3. In a society where disrespect for leaders is prevalent, how can you honor God with your thoughts and words towards His appointed leaders?

4. Write out a prayer of repentance for the dishonor you've shown God regarding the leaders in your life. Pray that the Spirit would empower you to overcome your flesh and to respect the authority over you.

## DIGGING DEEPER 10

**Acts 4:1-22**

1. Was Peter disrespectful when he answered the questions presented to him by the rulers, elders, and teachers of the law?

2. Verses 19 and 20 show Peter and John going directly against what the authorities told them to do. How does this situation compare to that of the Scriptures we previously discussed, Numbers 12 & 1 Samuel 24?

3. How will you know when to speak out and when to submit? Write a prayer in response to this question.

## DIGGING DEEPER 11

**1 Samuel 25:1-35**

1. Describe David's tone in verses 5-8.

2. What was Nabal's tone in verses 10 and 11?

3. What was David's initial response?

4. In verses 14-17, what action did a servant take when he saw his master being unwise? It could be said that this servant was out of place or creating dissension in the household. What is your opinion of his actions?

5. List each step that Abigail took in response to what the servant told her.

6. How did Abigail behave like a warrior, dedicated not merely to the rules, but to a higher cause? What were some of the "rules" Abigail broke in order to save her household?

7. Note the tone and carefully-chosen words Abigail used in speaking to David. Write down a few of the words and phrases that jump out at you.

8. Spend some moments in prayer asking the Spirit to help you apply the principles He's been teaching you through His Scripture.

# BATTLE PLAN

. . . . . . . . .

"By failing to prepare, you are preparing to fail."
Benjamin Franklin

ROLLING OVER SHE REACHES FOR THE BLARING ALARM CLOCK, AND THROUGH *her half-opened eyes she sees a small person peering at her from beside her bed. Giving a small smile she says, "Good morning, sweetheart."*

*"I'm hungry," declares the child.*

*"Mmmmmk," says the mama, swinging her legs over the side of the matress trying to push through the fog inside her brain.*

*Fussing starts oozing from the girl, setting the momma's heart to a faster beat. Pulling the child into bed and handing her a cell phone, she manages to keep the fussing at bay while exiting to go pee and gets some coffee.*

*Reaching into the fridge for cream, after pouring the delightful, warm black beverage, disappointment grips her at the realization that, while at the store yesterday, she'd forgotten half & half.*

*Scooping up her daughter, they load in the car and drive to the corner market. In she walks to the gas station, with some matted hair and a disheveled shirt, hoping her sunglasses cover up the mascara from yesterday that's smeared on the side of her eye.*

. . . . . . . .

*Swiping her debit card, ready to pay an exorbitantly large amount for this small container of cream, her card is declined. Remembering wryly that because of those overdraft fees, she had made sure that her card would get denied if there wasn't enough money in the account, her belly churned.*

*Slightly embarrassed, she finagles her credit card out of her wallet with one hand, holding onto her fussy, fidgety, and grabby daughter with the other hand. As soon as the clerk hands her the receipt, she takes her cream, and the donut she grabbed to keep her daughter quiet, and they head home.*

*Pouring cereal for her daughter back in the kitchen, she finally gets to sip her creamy, now-micro-waved beverage. Sighing and breathing in the smell of her coffee goodness, she glances at the calendar. Realizing she has an appointment in an hour she curses under her breath…*

Now, perhaps you don't have a child demanding things from you first thing in the morning, and maybe you don't care about having cream for your coffee, or perhaps you don't drink coffee at all, but I'm guessing that you can relate in some way to the story of this frazzled mama.

We all have experienced a day (or more!…) when we feel utterly unprepared.

The real problem occurs when we face *most* of our days unprepared.

God is a planner. Not all of us have been naturally gifted with this characteristic, but studies have proven that the most effective people are those who have a plan. Additionally, we have been instructed in 1 Corinthians 14 to desire and pursue all the spiritual gifts. We might not have the gift of administration, but pursuing it will bring us closer to being effective and powerful in both this world and eternity.

Enter our "Battle Plan."

I use this verbiage because we are talking about being a warrior. We know there is a spiritual battle happening all around us, all the time. But here's the thing: if we think about every day as a battle, we'll get exhausted. Who wants to constantly be on the offensive or defensive? That's not how God wants us to live. Instead, He wants us to live with the all-surpassing peace that He has made available for us. Having a plan allows us to be less aggressive, but it also motivates us past being passive. We peacefully (or determinedly) just take the next step, onto what we know comes next in the plan.

Now, I use the term "Battle Plan" because things like budgeting and meal planning are important, ladies. These types of plans have the power to make or break us on any given day.

If you want to be effective in the Kingdom of God, then you need to learn to be effective in your day and in your immediate environment. King David, even while he was "just" a shepherd, had a plan and a strategy. He took his work seriously, and because he was willing to apply every effort to shepherd his flock, protecting his sheep at all costs, he was later counted worthy to shepherd a nation.

The enemy has a strategic plan to keep you from being great every day. He knows your weaknesses, and he knows exactly where to jab you to render you ineffective.

So, plan your days, ladies! The royal position you hold requires you to balance your time and responsibilities with honor. In order to do this well, you must first take seriously what is in front of you. Then apply yourself to it with a joyful heart and with your utmost, to do it well as unto Christ. This is where God has you today, in this season. Taking the time to create a strategy is an effective tool to become a successful Royal Warrior.

As you create your lists, plans, and budgets, you must consult with the King and be disciplined enough to put your hands to the work.

Be aware of the Spirit, though, as He may guide you down a different path as the day, month, or year goes on. He'll extend to you the grace to change things up when you feel like doing something different, or He might even call you in a completely different direction as opportunities present themselves. Be aware that you **will** hit bumps in the road -- a kid throws up, an unexpected bill arrives, a team member doesn't come through… Being equipped with the Spirit of power, love, and sound mind means you will be able to respond well in the face of unexpected roadblocks.

**When** you hit that inevitable bump in the road, consult with the King, and then make and follow plan B. Perhaps you'll even need a plan C. But God already knows, so have faith in our Commander, knowing that He sees all and is working in all, and He gives us freedom in our battle plans. Having confidence in our Commander motivates us with both the discipline to follow our plan, and the grace to know when we should veer away.

## DIGGING DEEPER 12

### 1 Chronicles 28:19 & 20

1. Has the Lord given you a work to do? What are the calls on your life right now? Take as much time as you need, hours or days or maybe even weeks, to prayerfully consider this. Just make sure you come back and write out your answer.

2. Do you have a plan to accomplish the work God has given you? If you have a plan, write it out. If you have no plan to accomplish the call God has placed on your life, make one now.

3. Post verse 20 in a prominent spot to motivate you to press toward the goal.

## DIGGING DEEPER 13

### Proverbs 21:29-31

1.  Would you consider yourself to be one who gives thoughts to her ways? Why?

2.  Is it a comfort to know that nothing can succeed against the Lord? As you plan for and proceed through your day, why is it good to keep verse 30 in mind?

3.  Verse 31 reveals what we are responsible for and what God is responsible for. Translate this verse into your own words and write it down.

4.  Compose a prayer in response to these verses.

## DIGGING DEEPER 14

### Psalm 106:13-14

1.  The consequences that came to the Israelites for not waiting on God's counsel (NLT) were extreme. What steps can you take to be sure that you don't move forward in any plan without God's guidance?

2.  Verse 14 says that the Israelites gave into their craving. Compose a prayer asking God to make you sensitive enough to His will that you would be able to sense the difference between a fleshly craving to move without Him versus a prompting of the Holy Spirit to move in a given direction.

## DIGGING DEEPER 15

### Proverbs 16:3 & 9

1.  I see three steps to take as we consider these verses:

    1)  Prayerfully commit your work to the Lord.
    2)  Prayerfully write out your plans.
    3)  Trust that the Lord will guard, guide, and make a way for you as you apply yourself to the very things you just wrote and prayed about.

    Remember these three steps the next time you write a list or make a plan.

2.  Write out verse 9 in your own words.

3. How does knowing that the Lord establishes your steps affect the way you plan? If you haven't had this mindset previously, how will this truth change your planning and execution of any given plan?

## DIGGING DEEPER 16

**Ephesians 1:11**

1. How do we know God is a planner?

2. Knowing that God works all the disasters and hindrances in our life in conformity with His will should give us peace each time we are confronted with one of those hindrances. Write a prayerful response, examining any and all pressures you feel pushing against you right now. Ask God to reveal to you any new course of action you need to take and in what areas you might need to update the plans you have.

# CHAPTER 4:

# PREPARING
# FOR BATTLE

. . . . . . . . . .

Soldiers prepare for battle on their training ground.
We prepare for battle on our knees.
Anna Pachinsky

BEFORE WE GO GALLIVANTING INTO OUR BATTLES WITH OUR
plan, it's crucial to suit up!

*"Finally be strong in the Lord and in his mighty power. Put on the full armor of God so that you can take your stand against the devil's schemes"* (Ephesians 6:10).

The word "stand" is used more than a few times in the passages at the end of Ephesians, and I thought it would be worthwhile to look into this word. The word "stand" in the Greek is "histēmi". The biblical usage of this word includes the following:

```
make firm, fix, establish, be kept intact, escape to safety, to uphold or
sustain the authority or force of anything, to set or place in balance,
to stand immovable, of the foundation of a building, continue safe and
sound, stand unharmed, stand ready or prepared, to be of a steadfast
mind, of quality, one who does not hesitate, does not waiver.
```

. . . . . . . . .

I look at this word and see the description of a strong and mighty warrior in my mind's eye. Paul says we can take a *histēmi* by putting on the armor of God.

Through my study and application of this Scripture, I've become increasingly aware that putting on the armor is not a magic formula, but rather a beautiful imagery that expresses what the book of Ephesians has already explained in detail.

Paul was imprisoned in Rome while writing this letter, and he was constantly seeing the Roman armor. It was good armor that provided practical defense against attack. It makes sense that Paul would use this illustration to make his teaching applicable to his readers.

Watchman Nee explains the book of Ephesians in the most brilliant way with his book *Sit, Walk, Stand*. He breaks down Paul's writing in the following way: the first three chapters of Ephesians are doctrinal, as they speak about our position in Christ. The rest of Ephesians is practical. Chapters 4-6:9 tell us about our life in the world, and then 6:10-24 speaks to our attitude toward the enemy. We **sit** with Christ ("And God raised us up with Christ and seated us with him in the heavenly realms in Christ Jesus." - Ephesians 2:6 NIV*)*, we **walk** in the world ("I therefore, the prisoner of the Lord, beseech you to walk worthy of the calling with which you were called…" - Ephesians 4:1 NKJ), and we **stand** against the Devil ("Put on the full armor of God, so that you can take your stand against the devil's schemes." - Ephesians 6:11 NIV).

If we were to apply the book of Ephesians to the armor of God, we see that we were given the gift of truth (belt) and righteousness (breastplate), for which we **sat** and extended no effort at all to receive. Then we are responsible to bind on our peace (shoes), lift up our faith (shield), and **walk** out the joy of our salvation (helmet). Finally, we are to use the Word of God (sword) to **stand** and defeat anything that comes against us.

The exercise of daily praying my armor on has been monumental in my growth. As I've applied myself to this practice, I've broken free from a whole gamut of chains and bonds that I had no idea were holding me down.

The armor is a great tool that covers many bases as we seek to be spiritually successful. Its imagery is practical and provides a thorough prayer guide. The armor is something we must take responsibility to put on, and prayer is the way to do that. This is a way to live life full and free, in victory! Be prepared for the battles of each day by dressing yourself in full armor. It has been said that "prayer is the best armor against all trials."

## DIGGING DEEPER 17

### Ephesians

1. Read the book of Ephesians. Underline and then research anything that intrigues you. Take notes and write out any verses that speak to you.

## DIGGING DEEPER 18

### Ephesians 6:10-13

1. How can we be strong?

2. Why should we put on the full armor of God?

3. This passage lists one thing we **don't** struggle against and four areas where we actually **do**. What do we often believe that we struggle against but really don't? List out the four things against which we really do struggle.

4. Compose a prayer asking the Lord to reveal the areas in your life where you need to take a firmer stance. Ask God to show you what it looks like for you to stand against the devil in the season you're in right now.

## DIGGING DEEPER 19

### Ephesians 6:14

1. "The belt of truth around your waist…" Another term for "waist" is "core". Without the stability of a healthy core, every other movement is compromised. This is true both physically and also mentally/emotionally. Our behavior and thoughts stem from our core beliefs. Write out at least 4 core values you hold to in your life. Then write out at least 4 core beliefs.

2. Compare your core values and beliefs with the truth in God's Word. Make sure that each of the things you listed is centered in God's truth. Use Scripture to support each value and belief, writing out the verses or at least their references. Knowing your core beliefs and values well will help you establish all your thoughts and actions in truth.

3. Proverbs 4:23 states, "Above all else guard your heart, for everything you do flows from it." (NIV) How can righteousness guard your heart?

4. Please make a note of *whose* righteousness is the breastplate that guards your heart. Compose a prayer thanking God for the gift of His righteousness and petition for His help to choose rightly, resting in HIS righteousness and not your own.

## DIGGING DEEPER 20
••••••••••••••••••••••••••••••••••••••••••••••••

### Ephesians 6:15

1. The NASB version of this verse says "and having shod your feet…". The word "shod" in Greek means "to bind under one's feet". We are instructed here to wrap our feet with the preparedness of the gospel of peace. Write out what you think it means to be prepared with the gospel of peace.

2. Find three other Scriptures that pertain to the peace of God and write them out.

3. Compose a prayer thanking God for His gift of peace. Then petition that He would reveal more of it to you.

## DIGGING DEEPER 21
••••••••••••••••••••••••••••••••••••••••••••••••

### Ephesians 6:16

1. There are many interesting facts about the Roman shields during biblical times. These shields were very large and covered most of a soldier's body, they were covered in a leather that could be doused with water to put out any flames that came their way, and they linked with other shields to form a more impenetrable defense. Write out any parallels you see between a believer's faith and a Roman shield.

2. Describe how the enemy's lies can be compared to flaming arrows.

## DIGGING DEEPER 22
••••••••••••••••••••••••••••••••••••••••••••••••

### Ephesians 6:17

1. How does a helmet protect your head the way salvation protects your mind?

2. The Roman helmet had large dressings on top, which were there to make the soldier look larger and more threatening. When we have the salvation of God covering our heads, how is it possible to appear better than we actually are?

••••••••••

3. The "word" in verse 17 is "rhēma" in Greek. The biblical use of this word is "that which is or has been uttered by the living voice, thing spoken," (BlueLetterBible.com). This tells me that God's Word becomes as effective as a sword when it is spoken out loud. When you pray on your armor in the morning, make a point to do so out loud, rather than quietly in your head.

4. It is only through the prompting of the Holy Spirit that we know when to use Scripture and God's truth in the daily ins and outs of our lives. To wield the sword of the Spirit, we must be diligent to know and study the Scriptures and also to listen to the urging God may give within us. Write out a prayer asking God to prompt you to use the truth from His Word in your daily conversations and struggles.

5. Read Matthew 4:1-11. How did Jesus defeat Satan with the sword of the Spirit? Do you believe you could do this, too?

## DIGGING DEEPER 23

### Ephesians 6:18

1. When, how, and for whom should we pray?

2. Along with praying, what other instruction have we been given in this verse? Why would Paul urge us to do this?

3. What do you believe about prayer?

# CHAPTER 6

# Running the Race

• . . . . . . . •

"And let us run with perseverance the race marked out for us,
fixing our eyes on Jesus, the pioneer and perfecter of faith."
Hebrews 12:1-2

I RAN A MARATHON BEFORE I WAS MARRIED. I'VE NEVER REALLY enjoyed running, but caring for my body has always been a priority. Without access to a gym, training for a marathon was a great way for me to employ some discipline and stay fit. Additionally, the peer pressure of a great friend with whom I was training was a great help to motivate me in this activity that I didn't really love.

The marathon was in San Francisco, California. The course took us through all kinds of terrain: flat roads by the bay and wharfs, and also a lot of hills by the Golden Gate Bridge and Golden Gate Park. Along the way, I was presented with a few obstacles. I broke out in hives on mile 1, so by mile 3 I was running with Benadryl in my system. Around mile 13, my left foot started throbbing and swelling.

Our spiritual life looks similar to a race course that takes us through different terrain, as we are met with all kinds of circumstances. As we approach the different seasons of life, it's crucial to realize that this race we are running is a marathon. This is no 5K. This race will last our lifetime, and the results will impact eternity. Friends, there will be a time to sprint and a time to walk.

Perseverance has been defined as "a steady persistence in a course of action, steadfastness in doing something despite difficulty or delay in achieving

. . . . . . . . .

success, a continued effort to do or achieve something despite difficulties, failure, or opposition" (Random House Dictionary). In light of this definition, I would say that following and applying the instruction in Hebrews 12 means moving forward. As long as we don't let trying circumstances take us out of the race, if we take the time to deal with obstacles so that we can continue in the course marked out for us, we are persevering. Let us consider Jesus, the way our Savior cared for Himself and others as He ran His human race. His actions were never rushed; His ways were steady as He moved toward His finish line.

I was diagnosed with severe hypothyroidism a few years ago. The season of discovering my illness and then recovering was slow going, and learning how to truly rest was crucial to my recovery.

It was in this season that I came to a much greater understanding of God's grace. My inability to run well forced me to lean into Him. His grace carried me, and I had to be okay with not being strong enough on my own. I saw this image of trying to run my race while hauling my four boys along with me, verbally pushing them and physically dragging them along this dusty trail. They were getting filthy and scuffed up. I was getting nowhere, and my exhaustion was not only going to destroy everything in my world but also kill me. This picture slowed me down. And when I did slow down, the scene changed. In this new picture, I was not in workout gear, sweaty and straining, but in more elegant attire. I was walking leisurely along this dirt road, holding a mug of coffee and smiling while conversing with the four children around me. They'd discover things along the path, eager to show me and tell me all about it. I was able to laugh and enjoy every bit of them. Although this picture is different than the one that comes to mind when I read Hebrews 12:1-3, I think it can be applied.

I knew that Jesus had come to give me a full life - wanting me to thrive, not just survive - so I changed my battle plan. It was time to look at the season I was in and consider the terrain. It takes discipline to slow down; in fact, sometimes it takes more discipline to slow down than to "keep up". Sometimes the things that ensnare us on our journey are sins of pride as we chase perfection and holiness, often in competition with our fellow runners.

Run *your* race, sister. Focus on the ground before you, feel inspired and encouraged by the other runners, but remember that they won't be able to "beat" you in your race, because God did not make your life, or my life, a competition. Others are running their own race and we can celebrate their successes - yes, even the ones they post on social media - just as we would want them to celebrate with us.

Warrior, strive to press on, enjoying and embracing the terrain God has put before you. This striving and embracing requires us to beat our bodies into submission. Practically speaking, this might mean working hard to keep up in spin class, or it might mean telling your body to be quiet and climb in bed mid-day to read a novel. Maybe it's doing the dishes, and maybe it's snuggling with a child. God has called us to run the race as if to win. You will need to pace yourself. Depending on the terrain, acting in the spirit of discipline will sometimes look like reaching out to say "yes" to the leader in church who's asking you to serve. Other times, it will mean beating down that people-pleasing desire and saying the word "no".

As we fix our eyes on Jesus, the author and finisher of our faith, we will be able to run with perseverance the race that is marked out for us. Our goal is progress, not perfection. Perfection is being with Jesus at the end. We run for the joy of being with Him in eternity - of finishing the race with a smile and an embrace from our proud Lord.

## DIGGING DEEPER 24

### Mark 4:35-41

1. What does Jesus say to His disciples in verse 35? Does He mention anything about perishing or not making it to the other side?

2. Jesus had been teaching from the boat that they took to cross the sea. They made no move to go to shore and gather any kind of provisions for the journey, but "took him along, just as he was." Then He fell asleep on a cushion in a rocking boat, and slept through the rocking and the waves that were breaking over the side of the boat, nearly swamping it. Why do you think Jesus slept so hard?

3. The disciples woke Jesus, not to ask for help, but mostly annoyed that He was sleeping while they were toiling to stay afloat. They hollered, "Don't you care if we drown?" Have you ever tried to stay afloat in the circumstantial storms of your life and then finally gone to Jesus, but you approach Him because you've been offended that He hasn't come to aid you sooner?

4. Why would Jesus reprimand His disciples? Was He disappointed that they were feeling fearful in the storm?

5. In these few verses, we get a picture of both Jesus' humanity and His deity. Compose a prayer in response to these verses.

## DIGGING DEEPER 25

### Luke 5:16

1. Why do you think Jesus would do this? List some possible reasons.

2. I prefer the New International Version of this verse. It says, "But Jesus often withdrew to lonely places and prayed." Is this something you practice? Why should we follow Jesus' example in doing this?

## DIGGING DEEPER 26

．．．．．．．．．．．．．．．．．．．．．．．．．．．．．．．．．．．．．．．．．．

### John 4:6

1. Have you ever considered Jesus's habits as a human and the ways that He prioritized the care of His body and soul? Record any observations from this verse and what you know about Jesus' life.

2. Recall a time when you were tired, but thought you must not sit down because God's work needed to be done. Does reading that Jesus got tired and sat down to rest, while still doing the Father's will for His life, give you a sense of relief? Prayerfully record your response.

## DIGGING DEEPER 27

．．．．．．．．．．．．．．．．．．．．．．．．．．．．．．．．．．．．．．．．．．

### John 11:35

1. Jesus had a human life that went through seasons, the same as you and me. He allowed Himself a moment to express the despair He felt. The next time your eyes get wet, remember that there is no shame in your tears. Jesus wept, too. Right now, play a worship song and listen to the lyrics, resting in His presence. Be sure to thank Him for the season you are in and how He has given you freedom to experience and persevere in it through His grace. Feel free to mourn with pain if it is a wintery season *or* to rejoice if it is a summery season filled with fruit. Remember where He has brought you from.

## DIGGING DEEPER 28

．．．．．．．．．．．．．．．．．．．．．．．．．．．．．．．．．．．．．．．．．．

### Hebrews 12:1-3

1. In the race marked out for you, how would you describe your "terrain" at this moment? (Flat and smooth sailing? Hilly, providing just enough challenge? Rocky cliffs that are forcing slow, precise movement?)

2. Name the sin that might be entangling your run right now. Confess it to a trustworthy sister. Confession is a way to stop the entanglement.

．．．．．．．．．

3. How is Jesus the "pioneer and perfecter of faith"?

4. Jesus endured because of the joy set before Him. How can you do the same? Envision the joy that is set before you - that is waiting for you at the end of your race. How does this vision help you endure the hardship of any given moment?

5. Write out a prayer focusing your eyes on the author and perfecter of your faith. Lean into Him and make yourself available to hear how He wants you to persevere in your race today.

# CHAPTER 7:

# FROM VICTORY

. . . . . . . . . .

"If ever there comes a time when the women of the world
come together purely and simply for the benefit of mankind,
it will be a force such as the world has never known."
Matthew Arnold

ROYAL WARRIOR, YOU ARE VICTORIOUS. NOT BECAUSE YOU'VE
accomplished mighty things and overcome your troubles. Not because you beat your body into
submission and did all those hard things. You are victorious because God gave you victory. Because
you chose to believe and follow Jesus Christ.

**Before the beginning of time, you were successful and victorious**.

What motivates our movement should be the knowledge that we are fighting the enemy from a
place of ultimate victory. We do not need to fight *for* victory.

So then, there is no need to fear failure; in fact, there is no need to fear anything because Christ
has already won it all.

We might then ask, "What is this for? Why do we apply ourselves to anything if God has done
and is going to do it all for us?"

Because God's plan is not to make spoiled brats.

His plan is to make us Warrior Queens.

If we choose pride, or choose to be ungrateful for the title we bear, then we will lose our ability
to be powerful.

. . . . . . . . .

I look at Lamentations chapter 1, and I see a picture of a woman who has lost all her power. This passage is actually a description of Jerusalem, but I look around our world and I see women just like this all over:

*"Jerusalem has sinned greatly and so has become unclean. All who honored her despise her, for they have all seen her naked; she groans and turns away. Her filthiness clung to her skirts; she did not consider her future. Her fall was astounding; there was none to comfort her. 'Look, Lord, on my affliction for the enemy has triumphed.'"*

*- Lamentations 1:8 & 9*

Ultimately, Jerusalem is victorious and yet, she's chosen not to walk in that victory. She doesn't care to fight for righteousness; instead, she groans and turns away. She's given up hope. She's given over her power to sin and the enemy. This is not God's will for any woman.

In contrast, as I picture the women we are anointed to be, *I see a woman waking in her room in a castle. Pushing back the lush covers and putting her feet onto the marble floor, she's ready to apply herself.*

*She's ready to walk in victory. By no means does she want to take advantage of God's grace. A woman of such high standing is confident in her ability to get the work done.*

*She's disciplined enough to not allow laziness, sin, stress, or shame push her around. She is a regal slave to righteousness, walking in power and freedom.*

*She doesn't fight for victory; she knows victory is already hers. She fights from victory, tenaciously in love with her God.*

*And after she's danced through her daily battles, she nestles in at night, knowing she walked well that day. Although she is never perfect, she walks alongside her Lord, who is perfect. She is confident in the lessons learned and the victories won in the day she just lived. She rests well, her spirit at peace, knowing she is well cared for.*

"In this world you will have trouble.

But take heart!

I have overcome the world."

-Jesus

(John 16:33)

*Crown & Sword* Part 1 ch.2 "Be the Clay"
Phyllis McKee "Clay and Pottery." Infoplease.
© 2000-2017 Sandbox Networks, Inc., publishing as Infoplease.
18 May. 2017 <https://www.infoplease.com/clay-and-pottery/>.

*Crown & Sword* Part 1,ch.4 "In Walks Iniquity"
Iniquity; Powered by Oxford Dictionaries · © Oxford University Press · Translation by Bing Translator

*Crown & Sword* Part 1,ch.6 "Other Jars"
Pressfield, Steven. *The War of Art: Break through the Blocks and Win Your Inner Creative Battles.* New York: Black Irish Entertainment, 2012. N. pag. Print.

*Crown & Sword* Part 2,ch.1 "Claiming Power" D.D. 4
Beth Moore "Believing God", Published by LifeWay Press, © 2002 Beth Moore
Fifth printing April 2005.Reprinted and used by permission

*Crown & Sword* P2, ch.3 "The Enemy"
Jeremiah, David, Dr. "Lesson 1, Are We Really in a War?" *Spiritual Warfare, Terms of Engagement.* Atlanta, GA: Walk Thru the Bible Ministries, 1995. 14. Print.
( Cited from Craig Childs, *The Animal Dialogues* (New York: Little, Brown and Co., 2007); *The Week* (2-8-08), 40-41)

*Crown & Sword* P.2, ch.3 "The Enemy"
Kleptomaniac - message by Havilah Cunnington
http://truthtotable.com
http://havilahcunnington.com/
http://moralrevolution.com/

*Crown & Sword* P.2, ch 6 "Obedience"
Chambers, Oswald. "November 14." *My Utmost for His Highest: The Classic Daily Devotional.* Uhrichsville, OH: Barbour, 2015. N. pag. Print.

*Crown & Sword* P.2, ch.7 "The Kingdom"
"I Do Hard Things" by Havilah Cunnington, San Bernardino, CA 2014. p. 84-85. Print

*Crown & Sword* P.3, ch.1 "Agape"
Pretense. N.D. online Powered by Oxford Dictionaries · © Oxford University Press · Translation by Bing Translator

*Crown & Sword* P.3, ch.3 "Brotherly Love"
American Psychological Association (APA):

coheir. (n.d.). *Collins English Dictionary - Complete & Unabridged 10th Edition*. Retrieved May 19, 2017 from Dictionary.com website http://www.dictionary.com/browse/coheir

*Crown & Sword* P.3, ch.3 "Brotherly Love"
Heir. American Heritage® Dictionary of the English Language, Fifth Edition. Copyright © 2016 by Houghton Mifflin Harcourt Publishing Company. Published by Houghton Mifflin Harcourt Publishing Company. All rights reserved

*Crown & Sword* P.3, ch.4 "Eros Love"
http.//www.newworldencyclopidia.org/entry/Agape
"New World Encyclopedia:Agape." *New World Encyclopedia*, . 27 Jun 2009, 11:12 UTC. 19 May 2017, 19:58<http://www.newworldencyclopedia.org/p/index.php?title=New_World_Encyclopedia:Terms_of_Use&oldid=943147>. Pa 5, eros

*Crown & Sword* P.3, ch.4 "Eros Love"
Lewis, C. S. *The Four Loves: The Voice and Words of C.S. Lewis*. Rec. 1960. Parish of the Air/Episcopal Radio-TV Foundation, n.d. CD.

*Crown & Sword* P.3, ch. 4, "Eros Love" DD. 15
Ravish. (n.d.) retrieved at https://www.bing.com/search?q=ravish&form=EDGEAR&qs=P-F&cvid=03bcb639765f4ad2af6e045fe2df0f8f&cc=US&setlang=en-US
Powered by Oxford Dictionaries · © Oxford University Press

*Crown & Sword* P.3, ch.5 "Princess Bride" DD17
"Redeemer." *Merriam-Webster.com*. Merriam-Webster, nd. Web. 19 May 2017.

*Crown & Sword* P.3, ch.5 "Princess Bride" DD18, DD19
Nee, Watchman. "The Initial Pursuit and Satisfaction." *The Song of Songs, The Divine Romance Between God and Man*. First ed. Anaheim,: Living Stream Ministry, 1995. 28, 29,119,121. Print.

*Crown & Sword* P.3, ch.5 "Storge Love"
Lewis, C. S. *The Four Loves: The Voice and Words of C.S. Lewis*. Rec. 1960. Parish of the Air/Episcopal Radio-TV Foundation, n.d. CD.

*Crown & Sword* P.3, ch.7 "Encountering the King" DD25
"Compassion." *Merriam-Webster.com*. Merriam-Webster, n.d. Web. 19 May 2017.

*Crown & Sword* P.4, ch.1 "Warriors are Disciplined"
warrior. Dictionary.com. *Dictionary.com Unabridged*. Random House, Inc. http://www.dictionary.com/browse/warrior (accessed: May 19, 2017).

*Crown & Sword* P4, ch.1 "Warriors are Disciplined"

GIRLS WITH SWORDS PUBLISHED BY WATERBROOK PRESS, 12265 Oracle Boulevard, Suite 200, Colorado Springs, Colorado 80921

*Crown & Sword* P.4, ch.1 "Warriors are Disciplined" DD3
"Lions" Text is available under the Creative Commons Attribution-ShareAlike License; Wikipedia® is a registered trademark of the Wikimedia Foundation, Inc., a non-profit organization.

*Crown & Sword* P.4 ch.2 "The Meek Warrior"
Bevere, Lisa. *Girls with Swords: How to Carry Your Cross like a Hero*. Waterville: Christian Large Print, 2014. Print.

*Crown & Sword* P.4, ch.5 "Preparing for Battle"
Nee, Watchman. *Sit, Walk, Stand*. Anaheim, CA: Living Stream Ministry, 1993. Print.

*Crown & Sword* P.4, ch.6 "Running the Race"
Perseverance. *Random House Unabridged Dictionary,* Copyright © 1997, by Random House, Inc., on Infoplease.